Build Your Own Wood Toys

R. J. DeCristoforo

 Sterling Publishing Co., Inc. New York

Library of Congress Cataloging-in-Publication Data

DeCristoforo, R. J.
    Build your own wood toys / R. J. DeCristoforo.
      p. cm.
    Abridged reprint of: Build your own wood toys, gifts & furniture.
  c1981.
    Includes index.
    ISBN 0-8069-6993-8
    1. Wooden toy making.   I. Title.
  TT174.5.W6D44   1989
  745.592—dc18 —dc19   88-33364
                                                         CIP

3 5 7 9 10 8 6 4 2

Published in 1989 by Sterling Publishing Co., Inc.
387 Park Avenue South, New York, N.Y. 10016
The material in this book was originally published by Grolier Book Clubs, Inc.,
in "Build Your Own Wood Toys, Gifts & Furniture"
© 1981 by R. J. DeCristoforo
Distributed in Canada by Sterling Publishing
℅ Canadian Manda Group, P.O. Box 920, Station U
Toronto, Ontario, Canada M8Z 5P9
Distributed in Great Britain and Europe by Cassell PLC
Artillery House, Artillery Row, London SW1P 1RT, England
Distributed in Australia by Capricorn Ltd.
P.O. Box 665, Lane Cove, NSW 2066
Manufactured in the United States of America
All rights reserved

Sterling ISBN 0-8069-6993-8 Paper

For all the children—
and the grownups too

Contents

Metric Conversion Chart   viii
Preface   ix

I. Project Essentials

Materials and Tools   3

II. Mainly for Kids: Toys

Wheels and Axles   67

Basic Pull Toys

project 1:	Puppy Pull Toy	96
project 2:	Hippo Pull Toy	101
project 3:	Whale of a Pull	102
project 4:	Spotty Dog	103
project 5:	Drag a Dragon	104
project 6:	Toting Dachshund	106

Pull Toys with Action

project 7:	Hopping Bunny Pull Toy	110
project 8:	Walking Ducks Pull Toy	114
project 9:	Dog with Waggly Ears	120
project 10:	Elephant with Nodding Head	124
project 11:	Rolling Drum Push or Pull Toy	128
project 12:	Push or Pull Ferris Wheel	132
project 13:	Pinwheel Pull Toy	140
project 14:	Swiveling Crocodile	144

Trucks and Cars

project 15: Cab   148
project 16: Log Carrier   152
project 17: Moving Van   154
project 18: Sand Carrier   158
project 19: Bug   162
project 20: Sports Car   166
project 21: Bus   168

On-Track Train

project 22: Locomotive   170
project 23: Passenger Cars   174
project 24: Track   176

The Train

project 25: Locomotive   178
project 26: Tender   182

Games

project 27: Tick-Tack-Toe Board and Men   184
project 28: Single Post   190
project 29: Triple Post   193
project 30: Spiral Game   196
project 31: Zig-Zag Traveler   200
project 32: Marble Ride   204
project 33: Marble Roller Coaster   212

Wagons

project 34: Toy-Tote Wagon   222
project 35: Express Wagon   228

Riding Toys

project 36: Kiddie Car   238
project 37: Rocking Horse   246

project 38: No-Gas Car   256

Index   274

METRIC EQUIVALENCY CHART

MM—MILLIMETRES   CM—CENTIMETRES

INCHES TO MILLIMETRES AND CENTIMETRES

INCHES	MM	CM	INCHES	CM	INCHES	CM
1/8	3	0.3	9	22.9	30	76.2
1/4	6	0.6	10	25.4	31	78.7
3/8	10	1.0	11	27.9	32	81.3
1/2	13	1.3	12	30.5	33	83.8
5/8	16	1.6	13	33.0	34	86.4
3/4	19	1.9	14	35.6	35	88.9
7/8	22	2.2	15	38.1	36	91.4
1	25	2.5	16	40.6	37	94.0
1 1/4	32	3.2	17	43.2	38	96.5
1 1/2	38	3.8	18	45.7	39	99.1
1 3/4	44	4.4	19	48.3	40	101.6
2	51	5.1	20	50.8	41	104.1
2 1/2	64	6.4	21	53.3	42	106.7
3	76	7.6	22	55.9	43	109.2
3 1/2	89	8.9	23	58.4	44	111.8
4	102	10.2	24	61.0	45	114.3
4 1/2	114	11.4	25	63.5	46	116.8
5	127	12.7	26	66.0	47	119.4
6	152	15.2	27	68.6	48	121.9
7	178	17.8	28	71.1	49	124.5
8	203	20.3	29	73.7	50	127.0

YARDS TO METRES

YARDS	METRES	YARDS	METRES	YARDS	METRES	YARDS	METRES	YARDS	METRES
1/8	0.11	2 1/8	1.94	4 1/8	3.77	6 1/8	5.60	8 1/8	7.43
1/4	0.23	2 1/4	2.06	4 1/4	3.89	6 1/4	5.72	8 1/4	7.54
3/8	0.34	2 3/8	2.17	4 3/8	4.00	6 3/8	5.83	8 3/8	7.66
1/2	0.46	2 1/2	2.29	4 1/2	4.11	6 1/2	5.94	8 1/2	7.77
5/8	0.57	2 5/8	2.40	4 5/8	4.23	6 5/8	6.06	8 5/8	7.89
3/4	0.69	2 3/4	2.51	4 3/4	4.34	6 3/4	6.17	8 3/4	8.00
7/8	0.80	2 7/8	2.63	4 7/8	4.46	6 7/8	6.29	8 7/8	8.12
1	0.91	3	2.74	5	4.57	7	6.40	9	8.23
1 1/8	1.03	3 1/8	2.86	5 1/8	4.69	7 1/8	6.52	9 1/8	8.34
1 1/4	1.14	3 1/4	2.97	5 1/4	4.80	7 1/4	6.63	9 1/4	8.46
1 3/8	1.26	3 3/8	3.09	5 3/8	4.91	7 3/8	6.74	9 3/8	8.57
1 1/2	1.37	3 1/2	3.20	5 1/2	5.03	7 1/2	6.86	9 1/2	8.69
1 5/8	1.49	3 5/8	3.31	5 5/8	5.14	7 5/8	6.97	9 5/8	8.80
1 3/4	1.60	3 3/4	3.43	5 3/4	5.26	7 3/4	7.09	9 3/4	8.92
1 7/8	1.71	3 7/8	3.54	5 7/8	5.37	7 7/8	7.20	9 7/8	9.03
2	1.83	4	3.66	6	5.49	8	7.32	10	9.14

Preface

This is a book of toy and game projects. Some can be completed in an evening; others require more time. Some projects are comparatively *easy* to build. But if you want the easier projects to show good craftsmanship, they will need the same attention and care as the *harder* projects.

The first section in this book has information on materials such as lumber, lumber products, and fastening hardware; information on dowels; tool techniques; and so on. Next come the toy and game projects. This section is introduced by a chapter showing the secrets for making a variety of wheels and axles—needed for most of the toys.

All drawings show full details and recommended measurements. You can transfer patterns to wood by using the enlarging-by-squares method. This method also allows you to change sizes of projects. For example, if the drawing recommends ½-inch squares, you can always opt for a larger version, using ¾- or 1-inch squares. Then too, it's not critical that a toy car be a certain length if you prefer a different length.

I've had each of the toys and games in this book child tested. And many items have also been market-tested. That is, they would likely sell if you made them for extra income.

The essential materials are wood and wood products. All projects can be made either with hand or power tools, which really only determine production time, not quality. After all, a carefully cut curve looks the same whether cut with a jigsaw or a coping saw. The occasional plastics included are items such as recycled caps from bottles and pens, and some decorative tapes. Nothing here needs a battery.

You can enjoy using some of the toy projects *with* children. There's a tick-tack-toe game with some extra functions. There's a spiral game that will test your coordination as well as a child's. There's a wagon for the child to pull and tote things in. And there's a wagon for *you* to pull when toting the child. A no-gas car will give you exercise, since you push it up a gentle slope after the child drives it down. Yet this car will be strong enough for *you* to ride in too—provided the child lets you.

Because children don't object to the natural look of wood, I gave the toy and game projects natural finishes. But that shouldn't stop you from substituting bright colors. If you do, be sure to work with non-toxic sealers and finishes.

In these days of save-a-dollar do-it-yourselfing, it's easy to forget the plain old fun that should be part of home workshop tasks. Of course, there's great satisfaction to be had in doing home chores you'd otherwise hire out for. But it's also smart to tackle projects just for the fun of doing them—and then perhaps for the added joy of giving the finished projects as gifts.

Since all projects in this book are for home and family, they'll offer you opportunities for family activities that can substitute for passive diversions such as television. I can vouch for the interest the toy and game projects arouse in children. In fact, kids seem *determined* to help build them.

You may be surprised at the tasks children can do if you offer encouragement and instruction. Here's a good opportunity to teach the use of a tool or to demonstrate, for example, the different results from sandpapering with and across wood grain. Kids don't need kids' tools, which are generally useless anyway and can lead to discouragement. Of course, you should adjust your expectations to the child's readiness. Some children learn quicker and handle tools better than other children of the same age. So you'll have to chose tools and determine your supervision accordingly. Yet it's common that a four- or five-year old can use a hand saw correctly. Not a full-size saw! A 12- to 14-inch saw will serve well. Such "short" saws are available individually, or they can be found in a "Nest of Saws" package. For kids, avoid use of a keyhole or compass type saw since these usually have dangerously sharp points.

Whatever the tool, kids can learn only what you teach. If you want them to help, want them to enjoy what they are doing, and want to enjoy them while they are doing it, remind yourself to be a patient teacher. Otherwise the whole proposition might be a mistake. Be sure that you and your helpers have fun. That's important.

R.J. De Cristoforo

I.
PROJECT ESSENTIALS

MATERIALS AND TOOLS

LUMBER

The materials used for the majority of the projects in this book are pine and fir lumber, good grades of plywood, some pieces of hardwood, and occasionally some hardboard. The materials lists that accompany many of the drawings do not always specify the wood species to use. They simply state "lumber" or "plywood." This allows you options.

Usually, birch can be used—in place of maple, for example, because they are both hardwoods. But a hardwood can't be substituted for a softwood.

And you shouldn't substitute lumber for plywood. Because you can make many of the projects in this book from small pieces, having a choice allows the use of suitable "scrap," that is, leftovers you previously couldn't bring yourself to discard or burn.

Wood is classified as *hardwood* or *softwood,* but the terms are not truly adequate since they are just forestry designations that tell whether the wood came from a broad-leaved, deciduous tree (hardwood) or a needle-bearing, evergreen tree (softwood). In each category the actual *working* hardness or softness of some particular species confutes the classification. For example, fir is a "softwood" that is quite hard. Poplar is a "hardwood" that is relatively soft and easy to work.

Pine, cedar, redwood, and fir are all softwoods. Mahogany and walnut (both easy to cut) and maple, birch, cherry, and oak are common hardwoods. Here are some factors that can influence your selection of wood.

Appearance. An elaborate, heirloom-type project, where material cost is not a factor, justifies an exotic species with an attractive grain and painstaking finishing that enhances the design.

Use. There is little point in using fine cabinet woods to make garage storage shelves. This principle also applies to particular components in a project. If the part isn't visible (such as a reinforcement piece), you can make it from a more economical grade of wood.

Part Size. When the width of a project part is greater than 11 inches, you may want to choose between gluing up slabs of lumber or working with plywood. Your choice can also be influenced by your tools. It's not difficult to cut and assemble lumber slabs if you have a table saw, a jointer, and plenty of clamps. Yet even if you have an elaborate shop, you may opt for plywood. There are plenty of good grades of plywood that won't make you feel you've compromised on the project's ultimate appearance.

Wear and Tear. Wooden wheels on a project like a wagon that will be used outdoors and may bear the weight of a passenger should be made of a tough wood such as maple, birch, or fir. The wheels on light-weight pull toys, of course, can be made of tough woods too, but pine and even some grades of plywood will do.

Personal Taste.   Then too, you might choose one wood species over others because you like its natural finish, so, if I recommend fine lumber and you decide to use plywood, that's your privilege.

BUYING LUMBER

Lumber grades indicate quality and tell you roughly the kind and number of blemishes and defects a board may contain.

Softwood Grades.   Although there are some differences in grading procedures, the three basic classifications for softwoods are *select, common,* and *structural.* Each classification has subgroups that indicate quality.

• In the *select* group, which is kiln dried, the A-clear is top of the line, being wood that is practically defect-free. The B-select will have some blemishes, but can still be used for a natural finish. C and D grades have defects that can be concealed with paint.

• In the *common* group, classes are by number, with number 1 being free of decay, splits, and warp. But number 1 is allowed to have blemishes and tight knots. Numbers 2, 3, 4, and 5 decrease in quality. Number 5 isn't good for much other than filler in rough construction.

• The *structural* group doesn't include lumber of use for projects in this book. Its grades include *construction, standard, utility,* and *economy.* Quality declines rapidly from *construction* grade to *economy.*

It's convenient that most lumberyards allow you to select your own wood. Often, you may decide upon a lesser, more economical grade because you can see the salvageable material in it. A lumberyard "shelving bin" may contain scraps and odd pieces of various grades at discount prices.

It pays to browse and then inspect for grain, knots, blemishes, and weight. For example, the heavier of two similar B- or C-grade pieces may contain more moisture. The moist, heavier piece would be less desirable. Yet if B- or C-grade pieces have no other defects, you may be able to cut A-select pieces from them.

As **Figure 1** shows, actual wood dimensions are less than the dimensions you order. That's because sizes are labeled in the *rough* dimensions rather than in actual *dressed* dimensions. Remember this when reading a materials list. If the part is listed as $1\frac{1}{2} \times 3\frac{1}{2}$ inches, what you need is a 2 × 4. This does not apply to lengths. If you order a board 6 or 8 or 10 feet long, that's what you will get.

Hardwood Grades. Hardwood grading differs from softwood grading. A piece of softwood is usually judged and graded as a whole after it has been dressed. Hardwood is examined in the rough and graded on the basis of the clear wood it contains, rather than on its store of defects.

• *Firsts* and *Seconds* in hardwood grades are commonly combined and labeled as FAS. The material is judged from the poor side—which should allow you to get clear cuttings most of the way through. Technically, you should be able to get clear wood that is a minimum of 6 inches wide and 8 feet long.

• *Selects* are the next step down. While defects are allowed on the back side, the good or "face" side should be clear in pieces measuring not less than 4 inches wide and 6 feet long.

• Two other grades that might be worth considering are number 1 and number 2 common. They usually contain so much waste that they are cut up to remove bad parts and sold as "shorts." But such small pieces can be utilized as small parts for projects.

Hardwood thicknesses are often labeled in quarter inches. For example, 4/4 (four-quarter stock) means 1 inch thick. 6/4 (six-quarter stock) means

Fig. 1. This chart shows the nominal and actual sizes of softwood lumber. The text explains hardwood dimensions.

End Sections	Nominal Size (what you order)	Actual Size (what you get in inches)
▭	1 X 2	$\frac{3}{4} \times 1\frac{1}{2}$
▭	1 X 3	$\frac{3}{4} \times 2\frac{1}{2}$
▭	1 X 4	$\frac{3}{4} \times 3\frac{1}{2}$
▭	1 X 5	$\frac{3}{4} \times 4\frac{1}{2}$
▭	1 X 6	$\frac{3}{4} \times 5\frac{1}{2}$
▭	1 X 8	$\frac{3}{4} \times 7\frac{1}{4}$
▭	1 X 10	$\frac{3}{4} \times 9\frac{1}{4}$
▭	1 X 12	$\frac{3}{4} \times 11\frac{1}{4}$
▯	2 X 2	$1\frac{1}{2} \times 1\frac{1}{2}$
▯	2 X 3	$1\frac{1}{2} \times 2\frac{1}{2}$
▭	2 X 4	$1\frac{1}{2} \times 3\frac{1}{2}$
▭	2 X 6	$1\frac{1}{2} \times 5\frac{1}{2}$
▭	2 X 8	$1\frac{1}{2} \times 7\frac{1}{4}$
▭	2 X 10	$1\frac{1}{2} \times 9\frac{1}{4}$
▭	2 X 12	$1\frac{1}{2} \times 11\frac{1}{4}$
▯	3 X 4	$2\frac{1}{2} \times 3\frac{1}{2}$
◻	4 X 4	$3\frac{1}{2} \times 3\frac{1}{2}$
◻	4 X 6	$3\frac{1}{2} \times 5\frac{1}{2}$
◻	6 X 6	$5\frac{1}{2} \times 5\frac{1}{2}$
◻	8 X 8	$7\frac{1}{2} \times 7\frac{1}{2}$

$1\frac{1}{2}$ inches. 12/4 (twelve-quarter stock) means 3 inches. These dimensions refer to the wood in the *rough* state. The material loses thickness when dried and dressed. In a local lumberyard that stocks hardwoods you'll be able to see and measure what you are buying. If you order through a catalog, the thicknesses of dressed hardwood will run approximately as follows: 1 inch (4/4) will be $\frac{3}{4}$ to $\frac{13}{16}$ inch. $1\frac{1}{2}$ inches (6/4) will be $1\frac{1}{4}$ to $1\frac{3}{8}$ inches, and so on. If your needs are specific, be sure to state that you are listing *finished* sizes.

PLYWOOD

As in lumber, these man-made panels can be either *hardwood* or *softwood*. The terms tell what materials were used as the surface veneers. Common softwood plywoods are Douglas fir, pine, redwood, and cedar. The variety of hardwoods is vast, ranging from mahogany and walnut to rosewood and teak.

The face veneer has everything to do with appearance, but the workability of the panel is determined chiefly by the panel's core. The cut edges on veneer-core plywood, especially the economical shop-grade panels, are difficult to finish. They will often have voids which should be filled if the edge is left exposed. Cabinet-grade, veneer-core plywoods have tighter cores, and voids are rare. After a good sanding and finishing job, an exposed edge-ply can serve as an element of design rather than an eyesore.

Lumber-core panels work almost like solid wood. The core is actually a slab of solid boards that are edge-glued and run parallel to the grain of the surface veneers. A second layer of veneer (called crossbanding) runs at right angles between the face veneers and the core. Because lumber-core panels essentially have a lumber edge, you should have little trouble smoothing and finishing, drilling for dowels, and shaping.

Whatever plywood you use and no matter whether you finish naturally or paint, be careful when handling plywood edges. They're a great source of splinters.

TOOLS AND TOOL HINTS

Measuring and Marking Devices. "Measure twice, cut once"—that's good advice. No matter how good your cut is, the joint or part won't be right if you're not accurate and if you haven't carefully marked the dimension point or line. People often place the measuring device flat on the work and mark by making a short, heavy line. A better way is to make a dot with the point of a sharp, hard pencil. Many rules have incised lines that make fine grooves for the point of the marker to slide in **(Figure 2)**. Use the dot system even if the instrument does not have grooves—it's more accurate.

Measurement points and lines can be drawn with a sharp pencil, but often when marking cut-lines you can be more accurate if you scribe with a knife **(Figure 3)**. A bonus feature here, if you score carefully a few times, is that the knife severs the surface fibers, and this results in a smoother edge when you saw. If the knife line is difficult to see, simply mark over it with a sharp pencil.

Fig. 2. Use a sharp, hard pencil to mark dimension points. A dot, rather than a short, heavy line, is more accurate.

Fig. 3. A knife makes a finer line than a pencil and, because it severs surface fibers, it invites smoother saw cuts.

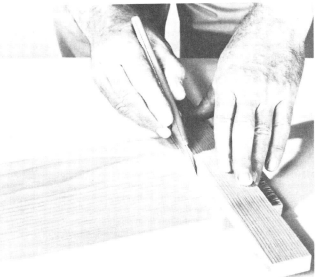

One of the more convenient measuring tools is a flexible *tape,* a palm-size instrument with a metal band that springs back into its small case when it is released. There are many types and sizes; some are very bulky, with tapes that stretch out to a hundred feet. In the shop, you'll want one that's easy to handle and read and measures at least 8 feet **(Figure 4).** That's the length of a standard plywood panel.

The *folding* or *zigzag* rule used to be the standby of the carpenter, and it's still popular, especially for short measurements. Most rules extend to 6 feet and are about 8 inches long when folded. Their stiff blades are an advantage. For example, they make a rigid span between the blade and rip fence on a table saw. Good ones have an extension, usually made of brass, that slides in a groove in the first blade **(Figure 5).** This makes it possible to use the rule for inside measurements. Because the sliding extension is removable, it can be used on its own as a small rule.

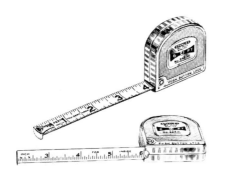

Fig. 4. A flexible tape is a convenient measuring device. Blades on shop types should be at least 8-feet long.

Fig. 5. The folding or *zig-zag* rule is still popular. The sliding extension can be removed and used as a short rule.

Fig. 6. Bench rules come in 1-, 2-, and 3-foot lengths. Good wooden ones have ends reinforced with metal.

A *bench rule* **(Figure 6)** is handy. It can be metal or hardwood, and is available in one-, two-, and three-foot lengths. It's a good measuring device and has an extra feature—it serves nicely as a straightedge.

A square is essential; the most useful one is the *combination square* **(Figure 7).** It has a removable, one-foot blade that can serve as a bench rule, and its head permits drawing lines square to an edge or at a 45-degree angle. The head can be locked at any point on the blade, which makes the combination square a good edge-marking gauge.

A pencil *compass* or wing *dividers* can be used to draw circles and arcs. Wing dividers are made with a removable steel point, so you can substitute a pencil when you need to. Tools of this type are limited in the radii they can

Fig. 7. The combination square has a 12-inch blade and a head that allows marking square across stock or at a 45-degree angle.

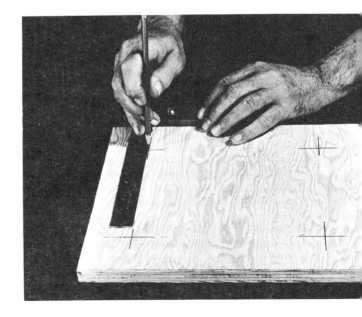

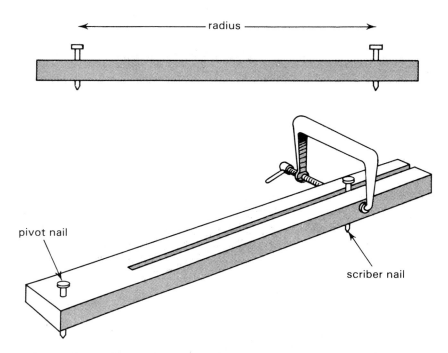

radius

pivot nail

scriber nail

Fig. 8. A design for making trammels to large circles. A bar 12 to 18 inches long will do for most work.

span; 6 inches is usually their limit. To draw larger circles you need special *trammels,* or you can work as shown in **Figure 8.** This trammel is an adjustable type—the scriber point can be locked with a small C-clamp at any point in the slot.

Saws. Hand saws **(Figure 9)** are designed either for *crosscutting* (cutting a board to length) or *ripping* (cutting a board to width). The major differences between the two types are the shape of the teeth and the number of them per inch on the blade. Rip saws have fewer, larger teeth with deep gullets between them for easy removal of large waste chips. Each tooth works like a tiny chisel, chipping out its own bit of wood.

Fig. 9. The teeth on hand saws are designed either for ripping or for crosscutting. The crosscut design is the better first saw to own.

Crosscut teeth cut with a shearing action; they cut across wood grain like so many small, sharp knives. The more teeth-per-inch on the blade, the smoother the cut will be. A good crosscut saw is a logical beginning for a hobbyist. It does a more respectable job of ripping than a rip saw does of crosscutting, and it is the saw to use for cutting plywood. Normally, a crosscut saw is stroked at about a 45-degree angle. Decrease the angle when you are sawing plywood.

In all cases, you will saw more accurately if you clamp or tack-nail a guide strip to the work as shown in **Figure 10.** The strip will help you to cut straight and to hold the saw vertical, creating an edge that will be square to adjacent surfaces.

A *backsaw* is very handy, especially when you are sawing small pieces and use the saw with a miter box such as the one shown in **Figure 11.** Common backsaws run about 12 to 14 inches long with many small teeth and a blade that is stiffened by a "spine" along the top edge. A good one is ideal for precise, straight or angled cuts. Construction details of a miter box you can make for yourself are shown in **Figure 12.**

Not all cuts are straight. Therefore, saws that can follow curved lines are essential, especially in toy-making. The *coping saw* **(Figure 13)** is a versatile saw designed for curve-cutting. Its U-shape frame has a chuck at each end for gripping blades that, on the average, are about 6 inches long. There are various blade widths with a wide assortment of teeth-per-inch specifications to match the work on hand. Choose a wide blade with large teeth for heavy stock; a narrow blade with many teeth is best for smoother cuts and intricate forms.

Because the coping saw's blades are gripped at each end, the saw can be used for "piercing" cuts—cuts made without need of a lead-in cut from the

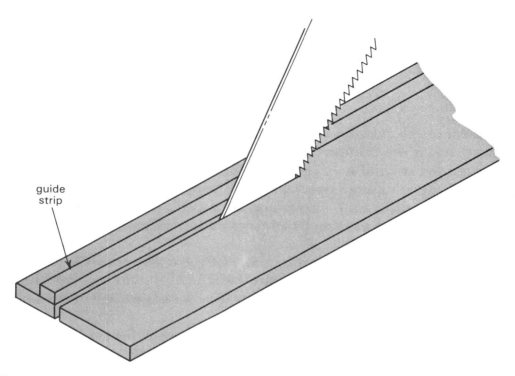

guide
strip

Fig. 10. Straight cuts will be more accurate if you tack-nail or clamp a guide strip to the work.

Fig. 11. A miter box helps you produce accurate straight or angular cuts. You can buy or make one.

Fig. 12. How to make a miter box: Use well-seasoned hardwood. Width of the box should suit the scope of work; minimum is about 4 inches. Assemble with glue and flathead screws. Mark cutlines accurately on edges and vertical surfaces before you saw. The accuracy of the box depends on how well you make the guide marks.

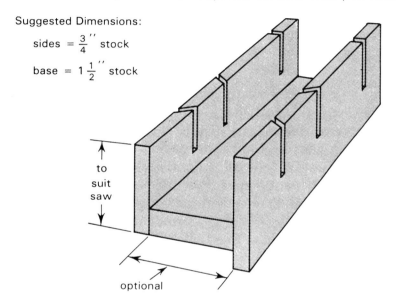

Suggested Dimensions:

$$\text{sides} = \frac{3}{4}'' \text{ stock}$$

$$\text{base} = 1\frac{1}{2}'' \text{ stock}$$

to suit saw

optional

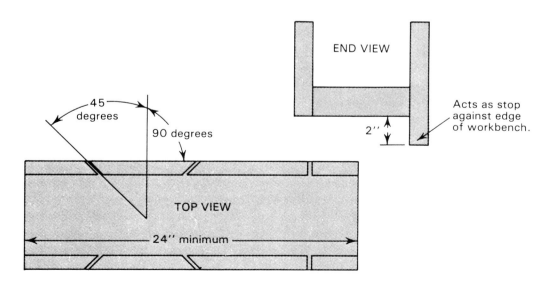

45 degrees

90 degrees

TOP VIEW

24'' minimum

END VIEW

Acts as stop against edge of workbench.

2''

Fig. 13. A typical coping saw. Some have deeper throats, but all have blade mounts that permit inside as well as outside cutting.

edge of the stock. To make a pierced cut, you first drill a hole in a waste area and pass the blade through before locking it in the chucks. The blades can be rotated in the frame, so the cutting direction can be adjusted to any line. Also, the blades can be installed so that the teeth point either toward or away from the handle. Thus you can conveniently saw on either the push or the pull stroke—handy for many types of work.

When you saw, the work itself should be firmly gripped, either in a vise **(Figure 14)** or on a special V-block holder that you can make for yourself **(Figure 15).** The holder can be clamped to a bench or gripped in a vise. It's a handy jig for holding work flat when you have a lot of coping work to do.

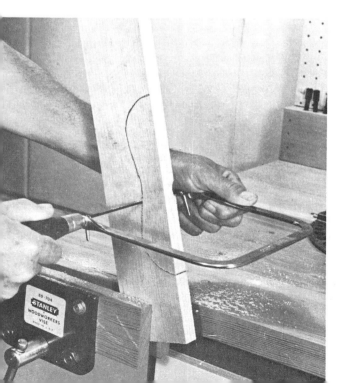

Fig. 14. Coping-saw blades can be rotated in the frame. They can also be mounted to cut on either the push or the pull stroke. The choice is often handy.

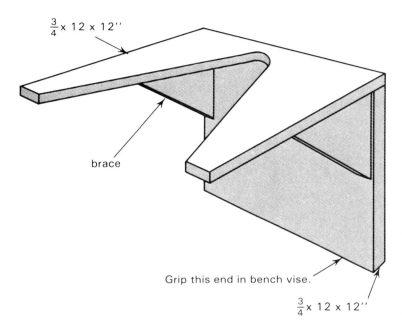

$\frac{3}{4}$ x 12 x 12''

brace

Grip this end in bench vise.

$\frac{3}{4}$ x 12 x 12''

Fig. 15. The V-block holder (details at left, supporting work below) is gripped in a vise. The work is clamped to its surface so the saw has freedom in the "V." Here, mount the blade so its teeth point toward the handle. Cut on the down stroke.

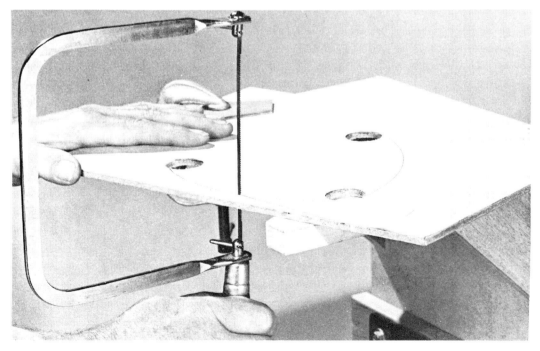

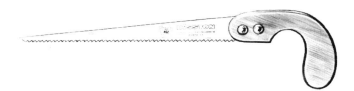

Fig. 16. The keyhole saw has a sharp point that allows you to start inside cuts by drilling a small hole in a waste area.

The *keyhole* saw **(Figure 16)** is also used for making external or internal curved cuts, but it can't do the fine work that is possible with a coping saw. An advantage of the keyhole saw is that the blade is "free." Thus you can make an internal cut much further away from an edge than with a framed saw.

The electric *saber saw* **(Figure 17)** is the tool to think about for easy curve cutting. It can do all the work of a keyhole saw and most of the work of a coping saw but much faster and with considerably less effort. Today's models have variable speeds and a large variety of blades, so tool applications can range from scrollwork to heavy-duty cutting.

Saber-saw blades are gripped only at one end. So, as shown in **Figure 18,** you can make internal cuts without a lead-in cut. The blade can be poked

Fig. 17.   The electric saber saw allows faster, easier cutting of curved lines. Modern ones have several or continuously variable speeds.

through a hole drilled in waste areas or it can penetrate the stock on its own with the following technique. Rest the saw on the front edge of the base so that the blade is parallel to the work surface. Hold the saw very firmly and slowly tilt it back until the blade makes contact and starts to cut a groove. Continue to tilt backwards until the blade has pierced the stock. Then you can set the tool firmly on its base and finish cutting.

Among stationary tools, the *jigsaw* (**Figure 19**) is the king of intricate curve-cutting. Like the coping saw, it has chucks that grip the blades at each end; piercing is possible when you pass the blade through a hole in the work and then lock the blade in place. The jigsaw handles well in delicate fretwork, but it's no sissy. Maximum depth-of-cut is usually about 2 inches,

Fig. 18. Shown below, inside cutting is easy with a saber saw. Just start the cut at a hole as explained in the text.

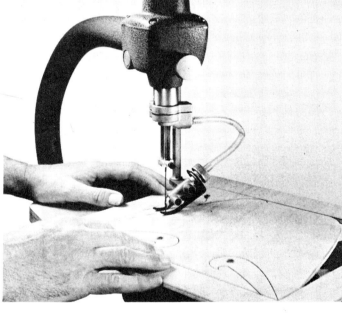

Fig. 19. Shown above, the stationary jigsaw is good for sawing all types of internal and external curves. A 2-inch depth-of-cut allows you to "pad," or stack, parts when you need similar pieces.

Blade	Blade Dimensions				Operation Facts		
	Thickness (Inches)	Width (Inches)	Teeth Per Inch	Stock Thickness (Inches)	Cut Radius	Kerf	Best for
5	.028	.250	7	$\frac{1}{4}$ and up	large	coarse	soft and hard wood, pressed wood
3	.020	.110	15	$\frac{1}{8}$ to $\frac{1}{2}$ in metal $\frac{1}{8}$ and up in other material	medium	medium	metal, wood, bone, felt, paper
1	.010	.040	18	$\frac{1}{16}$ to $\frac{1}{8}$	small	very fine	wood, bone, plastics
6	.012	.023	20	up to $\frac{1}{8}$	very small	fine	plastics, bone, fiber, comp. board
7	.020	.070	7	up to $\frac{1}{4}$	medium	medium	plastics, bone, hard rubber
8	.010	.070	14	$\frac{1}{8}$ to $\frac{1}{2}$	medium	very fine	wood, plastics, bone, hard rubber
2	.020	.110	20	$\frac{1}{16}$ to $\frac{1}{8}$	medium	medium	aluminum, copper, mild steel
4	.028	.250	20	$\frac{3}{32}$ to $\frac{1}{2}$ ($\frac{1}{4}$ max. in steel)	large	coarse	aluminum, copper, mild steel

Fig. 20. Common blades used in a jigsaw cut a variety of materials.

and it can accommodate blades as wide as $\frac{1}{4}$ inch for heavy-duty work. One advantage of the jigsaw is that you can get duplicate pieces. If, for example, a toy project needs two identical silhouettes, you can tack-nail or tape together two pieces of wood and cut them as if they were a solid piece. With a cutting depth of 2 inches, you can make a pad of eight pieces of $\frac{1}{4}$-inch plywood and have eight pieces exactly alike after a single cutting.

There are many types of blades available for jigsaws. **Figure 20** lists the most common ones and makes suggestions for their use.

Another type of jigsaw is the "Moto-Saw" shown in **Figure 21.** The tool weighs only 9 pounds, but has a 12-inch throat and can cut soft woods up to $1\frac{1}{2}$ inches thick. It's a comparatively quiet tool, so it's not impossible to think of using it in the house. Four rubber feet will keep the tool steady on most surfaces—it doesn't need a permanent mounting.

A *hacksaw* is needed to cut metal; for example, to shorten a bolt or to cut steel rod for an axle. The one shown in **Figure 22** can handle 10- or 12-inch blades. There are a variety of blades, but a $\frac{1}{2}$-inch-wide blade with 32 teeth per inch will be most useful.

Fig. 21. The "Moto-Saw" is a self-contained unit that weighs only 9 lbs. but can cut soft woods up to $1\frac{1}{2}$ inches thick. It can even be used on the kitchen table.

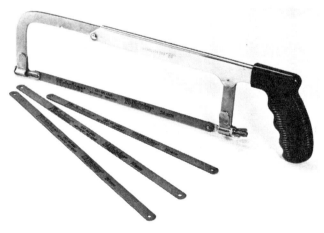

Fig. 22. The hacksaw is a metal cutting tool. It's handy for such jobs as cutting steel rods for axles or shortening bolts.

Hammers and Nails. A 16-ounce, curved *claw hammer* **(Figure 23)** is a good choice for general woodworking. It is not so light that it can't do a good job driving large nails, or so heavy that it becomes tiring and unwieldy. The one shown is a relatively modern version, having a steel handle and a vinyl grip. Some workers, especially those who work outdoors where steel feels colder than wood, prefer a wooden handle. The grip really doesn't matter as long as the tool is a good one. Hammers displayed in bargain bins are usually poor investments.

A small hammer, usually called a *tack hammer* **(Figure 24),** is a wise addition since it can be used to drive brads (small nails) as well as tacks. Some have heads that are magnetized—useful when what you are driving is too small to finger-hold.

A way to avoid damaging fingers when driving small nails is shown in **Figure 25.** The holder is just a strip of wood with a slot that is slim enough to grip the nail until you have it started.

The sizes and gauges of *common* and *box* nails are shown in **Figure 26.** Box nails are slimmer and are better to use when there is a chance that common nails might split the wood. In any case, if splitting becomes a nuisance on a particular piece of wood, it's a good idea to drill small pilot holes before driving the nails.

Don't drive nails so deep that the hammer head mars the wood. Just tap the heads flush.

Fig. 23. A 16 oz. curved claw hammer, for general woodworking. Good ones are also available with wood handles.

Fig. 24. A tack hammer is also good for driving brads. Some have striking areas that are magnetic to help you pick up and position tacks.

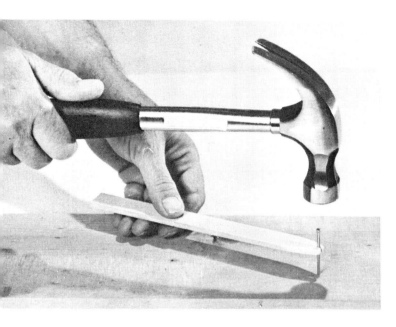

Fig. 25. Here's a device for starting a nail that is too small to conveniently finger-hold. The slot in the holder should be narrow enough to grip various nail diameters.

It's okay to use common or box nails when exposed nail heads don't matter; but if you wish to conceal the heads, switch to finishing nails **(Figure 27)**. The chart also lists "casing" nails. These are slightly heavier in gauge than finishing nails, and can be handy when you want a little more strength in a joint. They are frequently used by builders for cabinetwork and on interior trim.

Whether you use finishing or casing nails, the nail heads should be "set" below the surface of the wood, and the small hole that remains is filled with a wood putty, preferably one that is colored to match the wood.

Nail sets come in different sizes (the tips range from $\frac{1}{32}$ to $\frac{1}{8}$ inch in diameter). It's wise to have a set equal to the size of the nail, so that you won't have to make and fill holes larger than necessary.

The tool shown in **Figure 28** is a *self-centering* nail set. It's a handy gadget that makes nail-setting easier without marring adjacent surfaces. After the nail is driven to the point where you would use a conventional nail set (it should project about $\frac{1}{8}$ inch), place the tool over the nail and set it by striking the plunger.

COMMON AND BOX NAIL SIZES

Size d (penny)	2	3	4	5	6	7	8	9	10	12	16	20	30	40	50	60
Length in inches	1	$1\frac{1}{4}$	$1\frac{1}{2}$	$1\frac{3}{4}$	2	$2\frac{1}{4}$	$2\frac{1}{2}$	$2\frac{3}{4}$	3	$3\frac{1}{4}$	$3\frac{1}{2}$	4	$4\frac{1}{2}$	5	$5\frac{1}{2}$	6
Common Nails																
Gauge	15	14	$12\frac{1}{2}$	$12\frac{1}{2}$	$11\frac{1}{2}$	$11\frac{1}{2}$	$10\frac{1}{4}$	$10\frac{1}{4}$	9	9	8	6	5	4	3	2
Approximate number/lb.	845	540	290	250	165	150	100	90	65	60	45	30	20	17	13	10
Box Nails																
Gauge	$15\frac{1}{2}$	$14\frac{1}{2}$	14	14	$12\frac{1}{2}$	$12\frac{1}{2}$	$11\frac{1}{2}$	$11\frac{1}{2}$	$10\frac{1}{2}$	$10\frac{1}{2}$	10	9	9	8	—	—
Approximate number/lb	1010	635	473	406	236	210	145	132	94	88	71	52	46	35	—	—

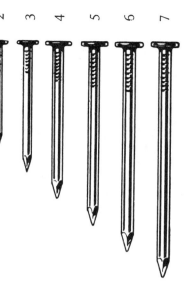

Fig. 26. This chart indicates actual lengths of *common* and *box* nails, though only common nails are shown. Box nails are slimmer but come in the same d (penny) lengths.

Fig. 27.   Facts and dimensions on finishing and casing nails and brads.

FINISHING-HEAD NAILS

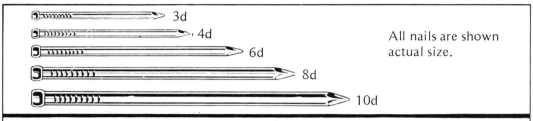

All nails are shown actual size.

FINISHING NAILS. These are used for decorative work where heads must be concealed or flush with the work surface. Some have cupped heads which make them easier to countersink and conceal with wood filler.

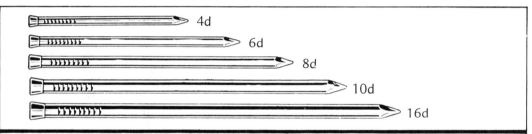

CASING NAILS. These are used mostly for interior trim and cabinetwork. Though slightly heavier in gauge than finishing nails, they are so similar that they are seldom stocked by retail dealers.

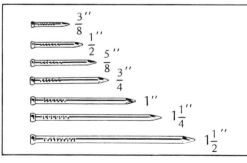

BRADS. These are smaller and thinner than finishing nails (16 to 20 gauge); they are used for light projects when heads must be concealed. Brads are sold by length rather than penny sizes in ¼- or 1-lb. boxes.

FINISHING NAILS					
Size	3d	4d	6d	8d	10d
Length	$1\frac{1}{3}''$	$1\frac{1}{2}''$	$2''$	$2\frac{1}{2}''$	$3''$
Gauge	$15\frac{1}{2}$	15	13	$12\frac{1}{2}$	$11\frac{1}{2}$
Quantity per lb.	875	600	309	196	125

CASING NAILS					
Size	4d	6d	8d	10d	16d
Length	$1\frac{1}{2}''$	$2''$	$2\frac{1}{2}''$	$3''$	$3\frac{1}{2}''$
Gauge	14	$12\frac{1}{2}$	$11\frac{1}{2}$	$10\frac{1}{2}$	10
Quantity per lb.	485	245	149	94	75

Fig. 28. A self-centering punch makes it easy to set finishing nails.

Fig. 29. This type of hand drill can be used for holes up to about $\frac{1}{4}$ inch. The hollow handle stores bits.

Don't drive nails as if you were trying for a prize in a carnival. Nails driven home with reasonable force will actually hold better, because they will cause the least amount of distortion in the wood fibers. Remove any nail that starts to bend. Even if you can save it, the bend may cause the point of the nail to travel crooked in the wood. It's better to use a new nail.

Drills. Small old-fashioned *hand drills,* those that work something like an egg beater **(Figure 29),** are still good for holes up to about $\frac{1}{4}$ inch. You can use them with small twist drills or special drill points such as those shown in **Figure 30.** Actually, heavy-duty versions with chuck jaws that can handle $\frac{3}{8}$-inch drills are available. Some have a "high" and "low" adjustment that allows you to choose extra torque or greater speed.

A *bit brace* **(Figure 31)** is the tool to use for hand-drilling holes $\frac{1}{4}$ inch and larger. They are available in light- and heavy-duty versions. The major difference between them is the diameter of the swing of the handle, called the "sweep." The greater the sweep, the more torque you can apply.

The chucks on most braces are specially designed to hold bits with tapered shanks, but some have universal jaws and can be used with straight shank bits up to $\frac{1}{2}$ inch as well. A good brace will have a rachet action that allows you to take full or partial swings either clockwise or counterclockwise. With a screwdriver bit, the reversing action allows you to remove screws as well as drive them.

Fig. 30.   Special sets of drill points for use in hand drills are available, but you can also work with small twist drills.

Fig. 31.   With correct cutting tools, the hand brace can be used to form holes as large as 3 inches. The gadget attached to the bit is an adjustable stop that lets you drill holes to a specific depth.

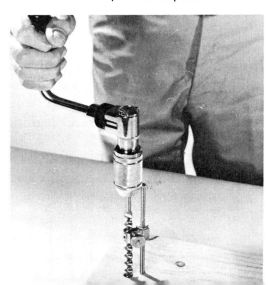

Fig. 32. Most hand braces are used with auger bits that have a tapered tang. Some have universal chucks so that they can also grip round-shank bits.

In **Figure 32** you see a typical *auger bit* that is used in a brace. The lead point is threaded to pull the bit into the work. Sizes of augers start at $\frac{1}{4}$ inch and increase by sixteenths to 1 inch. Numbers are often used to indicate bit size. For example, a number 9 bit will form a $\frac{9}{16}$-inch diameter hole.

The difference between brace auger bits and those that can be used in a drill press, for example, is shown in **Figure 33.** Never use a screw-tip bit for power drilling.

Fig. 33. Hand brace bits have a feed-screw point that pulls the bit into the work. They should not be used with power drills. Bits with brad points are safe to use with power tools.

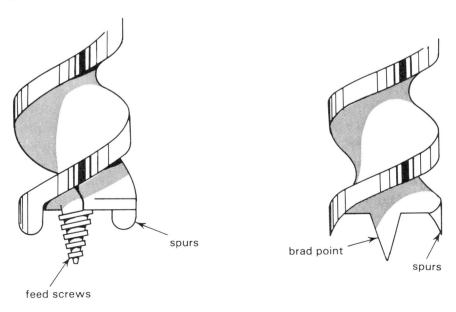

spurs

feed screws

brad point

spurs

Fig. 34. Expansion, or expansive, bits are designed for cutting large holes. Cutters are adjustable to allow you to bore odd-size holes.

Expansive, or *expansion bits* as they are sometimes called, are used to form holes larger than 1 inch. Most come with two cutters **(Figure 34),** and it's wise to work with the smallest one that serves the job at hand. Commonly, two sizes are available: one for holes from $\frac{5}{8}$ to $1\frac{3}{4}$ inches, the other for holes from $\frac{7}{8}$ to 3 inches. An advantage of this type of tool is that the cutters are infinitely adjustable, so you can form odd-diameter holes. It's feasible, for example, to bore a hole that falls between $\frac{3}{4}$ and $\frac{13}{16}$ inch.

Both types of bits are rather long; you can form deeper holes than possible with, say, a regular twist drill. Bit extensions that run from 12 to 18 inches long can do such jobs as boring cord holes through tall wooden lamp bases.

The portable *electric drill* is one of the tools that practically revolutionized homeshop woodworking. Few tool chests today lack one. It can do all the jobs of hand drills faster and easier, and, just as important, it can be equipped with accessories for jobs that range from sawing to sanding. Features on today's electric drills include double-insulation, variable speeds, and forward or reverse chuck actions.

Common electric-drill sizes are $\frac{1}{4}$, $\frac{3}{8}$, and $\frac{1}{2}$ inch. The fraction indicates the maximum chuck opening—but not necessarily the largest hole you can drill. Some drilling tools, like spade bits which can form holes up to $1\frac{1}{2}$ inches, have shank sizes that can be gripped in small drills. Spade bits are good tools for electric drills because they operate best at high speeds. Thus they can be used even in a "small" $\frac{1}{4}$-inch drill.

Generally, drill size indicates power and speed. A $\frac{1}{2}$-inch drill will have more torque but less speed than either a $\frac{3}{8}$- or $\frac{1}{4}$-inch drill. This makes sense, because the larger tool must stand up under heavy-duty functions such as drilling in steel or concrete. A $\frac{3}{8}$-inch drill is an acceptable compromise since its top speed is adequate for small-hole drilling and it has power for some big jobs. In truth, it's good to have both a $\frac{3}{8}$-inch drill and a $\frac{1}{4}$-inch version for general woodworking.

The portable drills are designed for hand use, but you can set them up like a drill press by acquiring a stand like the ones shown in **Figure 35.** These can be a great convenience on many jobs. Most important, they eliminate the chance of human error when it's critical for a hole to be perpendicular in the wood.

For accuracy when drilling, mark lines that intersect where the hole must be. Then use a punch or an awl to make a small indentation at the intersec-

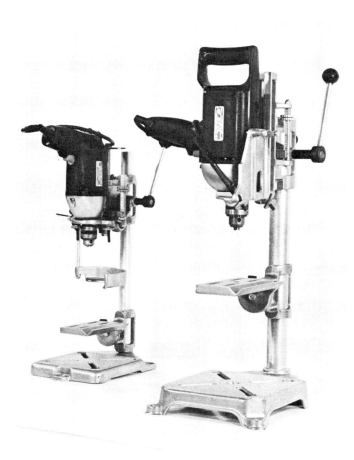

Fig. 35. Special stands are available for most of the electric drills on the market. A portable drill on a drill press allows accurate work.

Fig. 36. For accurate drilling, draw lines that intersect where the hole will be. Then punch a point at the center to help guide the drill at the start.

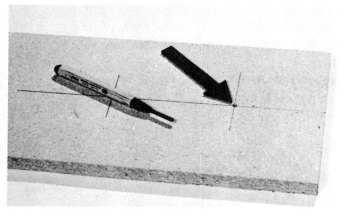

Fig. 37. The indentation forms a seat for the point of the bit, so it can't wander off. It also makes hole starting easier.

tion (**Figure 36**). This makes it easy to seat the bit accurately and start the hole (**Figure 37**).

Often it's a good idea to drill a pilot hole first. A pilot hole is a smaller hole than the final one you need. This makes drilling easier, increases accuracy, and results in cleaner holes. Always use a backup block when the hole must go through the work. This will minimize, if not eliminate, feathering and splintering where the bit comes through.

A small guide block such as the one shown in **Figure 38** can help you to drill squarely. When it is correctly sized, the guide block can also serve as a stop gauge when you are drilling to a specific depth. Another way to judge hole depth is simply to wrap a piece of masking tape around the bit (**Figure 39**). You stop drilling when the tape touches the work.

When a hole is required at a critical angle, use a guide block as shown in **Figure 40**. First drill the correct-size hole (or a pilot hole) through a square block of wood. Then saw off the base of the block so it will provide the correct angle, and use the block as a guide for the bit.

Figure 41 shows a secure jig you can make from a handscrew clamp for holding small parts while drilling. The matching V-cuts that are made in the jaws of the clamp will securely grip square or round pieces. The holder can be secured to a bench, held in a vise, or clamped to a drill-press table.

Figure 42 shows a similar way to do the same job. Here a conventional drill vise is used with a V-block to grip a small, round piece that requires a concentric hole. It's an accurate and safe way to work.

Fig. 38. A small guide block can help you to drill holes square to the surface. The block can also be sized to gauge holes of specific depth.

Fig. 39. Another way to drill to a predetermined depth is simply to wrap a piece of masking tape around the bit.

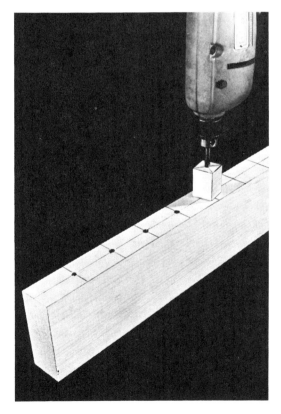

Fig. 40. Angular holes are difficult to "eyeball." It's better to work with a guide block like this one.

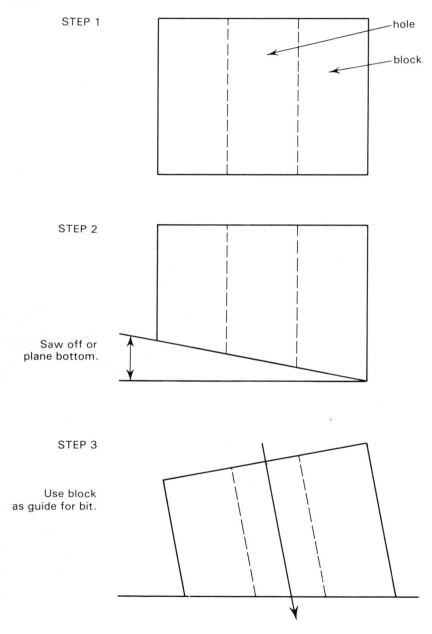

STEP 1

hole

block

STEP 2

Saw off or plane bottom.

STEP 3

Use block as guide for bit.

Fig. 41. Make matching V-cuts in the jaws of a handscrew and you have a tool that will securely grip small, square, or round pieces.

Fig. 42. A drill vise used with a V-block is one means for drilling straight, concentric holes through dowels and similarly shaped parts.

Screwdrivers and Screws. Conventional screwdrivers have a wing-type driving tip and are used to turn most of the common type of slotted-head screws used in woodworking: roundheads, ovalheads, and flatheads. Flatheads are often called "countersunk" screws because they are always driven flush with the work surface.

The efficient way to drive a screw is with a blade that closely fits the slot in the screw. Since there are many sizes of screws, it is good to buy the drivers in sets **(Figure 43)**. Using a small screwdriver to seat a 14 or 16 gauge screw is difficult, and will probably damage the tool.

The tool shown in **Figure 44** is a *spiral ratchet screwdriver*—a real time and labor saver. It automatically turns the screw when you push down on the handle. Most of these screwdrivers can drive or retract a screw or be locked in a fixed position for use as a conventional driver. They can be fitted with different-size blades for various screws. Incidentally, the tool's chuck will also grip drill bits—you can drill small holes quickly with it.

The tool shown in **Figure 45** is the kind of screwdriver bit that is used in a bit brace. Similar types, without the tapered shank, can be used in a

Fig. 43. The blade of a screwdriver should fit snugly in the screw-head slot. It's a good idea to buy these tools in large sets.

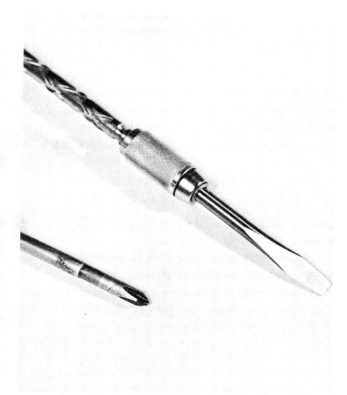

Fig. 44. You can drive or loosen screws faster and easier by working with a spiral-ratchet screwdriver. This tool can be used with various types and sizes of blades, as well as with small drill bits.

Fig. 45. Screwdriver blades like this big one, made in different styles and sizes, are also used in a hand brace.

portable electric drill. With a set of these blades and an electric drill with variable forward and reverse speeds, you would be well-equipped for most screwdriving chores.

Unless you are working with tiny screws and soft wood, you can drive screws easily and obtain maximum holding strength by drilling both a pilot and a shank hole **(Figure 46).** The depth of the shank hole can equal the full thickness of the top piece of wood being attached. The depth of the pilot hole should be about one-half the length of the threaded portion of the screw. Recommendations for sizes of pilot and shank holes are shown in **Figure 47.**

Fig. 46. Cross sections of two holes drilled for screws. The wood plugs that are inserted in holes for counterbored screws (below) are sanded smooth; the buttons leave a decorative touch.

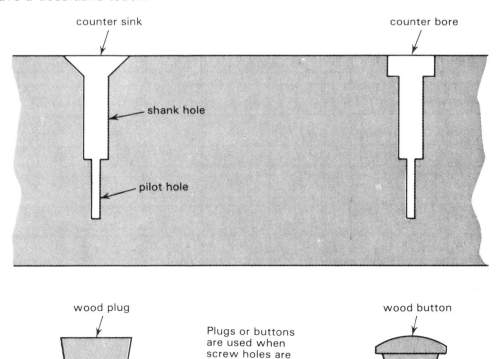

Fig. 47. If you follow these suggestions, wood screws will be easier to drive and will hold with maximum power.

HOLE SIZE RECOMMENDED FOR WOOD SCREWS							
	Pilot Holes				Shank Holes		Counterbore
Screw Number	Hardwood		Softwood		Twist Drill*	Drill Gauge**	Auger Bit Number
	Twist Drill*	Drill Gauge**	Twist Drill*	Drill Gauge**			
0	$\frac{1}{32}$	66	$\frac{1}{64}$	75	$\frac{1}{16}$	52	–
1	–	57	$\frac{1}{32}$	71	$\frac{5}{64}$	47	–
2	–	54	$\frac{1}{32}$	65	$\frac{3}{32}$	42	3
3	$\frac{1}{16}$	53	$\frac{3}{64}$	58	$\frac{7}{64}$	37	4
4	$\frac{1}{16}$	51	$\frac{3}{64}$	55	$\frac{7}{64}$	32	4
5	$\frac{5}{64}$	47	$\frac{1}{16}$	53	$\frac{1}{8}$	30	4
6	–	44	$\frac{1}{16}$	52	$\frac{9}{64}$	27	5
7	–	39	$\frac{1}{16}$	51	$\frac{5}{32}$	22	5
8	$\frac{7}{64}$	35	$\frac{5}{64}$	48	$\frac{11}{64}$	18	6
9	$\frac{7}{64}$	33	$\frac{5}{64}$	45	$\frac{3}{16}$	14	6
10	$\frac{1}{8}$	31	$\frac{3}{32}$	43	$\frac{3}{16}$	10	6
11	–	29	$\frac{3}{32}$	40	$\frac{13}{64}$	4	7
12	–	25	$\frac{7}{64}$	38	$\frac{7}{32}$	2	7
14	$\frac{3}{16}$	14	$\frac{7}{64}$	32	$\frac{1}{4}$	D	8
16	–	10	$\frac{9}{64}$	29	$\frac{17}{64}$	I	9
18	$\frac{13}{64}$	6	$\frac{9}{64}$	26	$\frac{19}{64}$	N	10
20	$\frac{7}{32}$	3	$\frac{11}{64}$	19	$\frac{21}{64}$	P	11
24	$\frac{1}{4}$	D	$\frac{3}{16}$	15	$\frac{3}{8}$	V	12

*nearest size in fractions of an inch
**this will provide maximum holding power

Fig. 48. Countersinks are used to form an inverted cone so that a flathead screw can be driven flush.

Countersinking, done with a spiral ratchet screwdriver in **Figure 48,** can be done after shank and pilot holes are drilled. Don't countersink to full depth if the wood is soft. Tightening the screw will bring it flush. Countersink to full depth if the wood is hard.

Usually, counterboring is done to conceal a screw. There are two ways to prepare the hole. Start with the pilot hole, then counterbore, and finally drill the shank hole or first do the counterbore, then the pilot hole, and finish with the shank hole.

Counterbored holes can be filled with short pieces of dowel or special wood plugs, both of which are sanded flush, or with decorative wood buttons. Both of these counterbore fillers are shown in **Figure 46.**

Whether you countersink or counterbore or do neither depends on the job you are doing and the design of the screw head **(Figure 49).** Flathead and ovalhead screws are always countersunk; the ovalhead requiring a shallower indentation than the flathead. The roundhead screw is often left exposed. Any of the screws can be concealed with either a plug or a button if you counterbore.

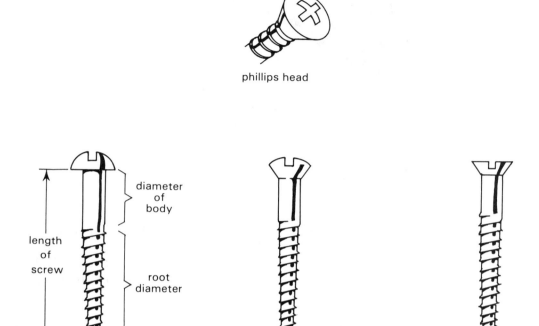

phillips head

diameter
of
body

length
of
screw

root
diameter

round head

oval head

flathead

Fig. 49. Common screw-head designs. The flathead and the oval head require countersinking.

Screw gauges and the lengths that are available in each category are shown in **Figure 50.**

Wood Plugs and Short Dowels. The cutter shown in **Figure 51** is used to make plugs for filling counterbored holes. The chamfered end that the cutter forms makes it easy to insert the plugs and also provides some room for excess glue. The cutter can pierce thin stock (up to about $\frac{1}{2}$ inch) and can be used to produce small, disc-type wooden parts. On thick stock you can cut to the full depth of the tool and then free the individual pieces by snapping them off with a screwdriver, as shown in **Figure 52.**

Fig. 50.   This shows gauges and lengths of wood screws. When you buy screws, specify the following: (1) length; (2) gauge number; (3) flat, round, or oval head; material such as brass, steel, bronze; (5) finish such as bright, steel blued, cadmium, nickel, or chromium.

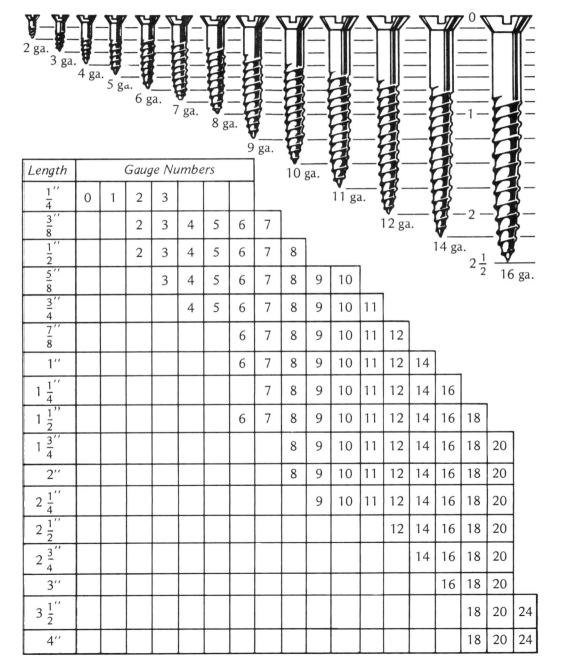

Length	Gauge Numbers																	
$\frac{1}{4}''$	0	1	2	3														
$\frac{3}{8}''$			2	3	4	5	6	7										
$\frac{1}{2}''$			2	3	4	5	6	7	8									
$\frac{5}{8}''$				3	4	5	6	7	8	9	10							
$\frac{3}{4}''$					4	5	6	7	8	9	10	11						
$\frac{7}{8}''$							6	7	8	9	10	11	12					
$1''$							6	7	8	9	10	11	12	14				
$1\frac{1}{4}''$								7	8	9	10	11	12	14	16			
$1\frac{1}{2}''$							6	7	8	9	10	11	12	14	16	18		
$1\frac{3}{4}''$									8	9	10	11	12	14	16	18	20	
$2''$									8	9	10	11	12	14	16	18	20	
$2\frac{1}{4}''$										9	10	11	12	14	16	18	20	
$2\frac{1}{2}''$													12	14	16	18	20	
$2\frac{3}{4}''$														14	16	18	20	
$3''$															16	18	20	
$3\frac{1}{2}''$																18	20	24
$4''$																18	20	24

Screw gauge labels (left to right, largest to smallest as drawn): 2 ga., 3 ga., 4 ga., 5 ga., 6 ga., 7 ga., 8 ga., 9 ga., 10 ga., 11 ga., 12 ga., 14 ga., 16 ga.

Length scale markings: 0, 1, 2, 2½

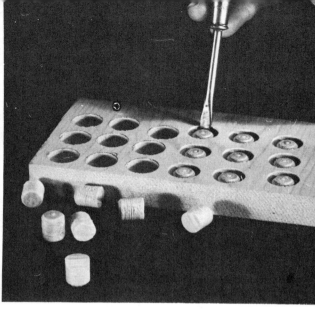

Fig. 51. This cutter forms the short plugs that are used in counterbored holes to conceal screws. The tool chamfers one end, and the plugs can be used like buttons.

Fig. 52. After drilling, snap the plugs off with a screwdriver. The boring tool (Fig. 51) can also be used to cut through material, but the stock can't be much more than $\frac{1}{2}$ inch thick.

If you use the plug to conceal a screw, insert it with the broken end out and then sand it flush with adjacent surfaces **(Figure 53)**. If the project calls for the plug to project (a decorative detail), insert it in the counterbored hole with the chamfered end up.

Fig. 53. When used to conceal, the plugs are inserted with the chamfered side down. Trim off excess with a knife or chisel, and then sand smooth.

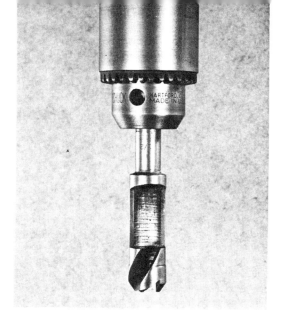

Fig. 54. This type of cutter can be used to form plugs, but it cuts deeper and can produce short dowels as well.

The tool shown in **Figure 54** is also called a plug cutter, but it can form dowels up to 2 inches long. An advantage of both tools is that you can form plugs and short dowels from material that matches wood you have used for the project; for example, pine plugs for a pine project. If you work very carefully you can match the plug's grain direction, even the grain pattern, to surrounding areas.

Don't use cutters like this with hand drills. You *might* be successful if you work with a portable electric drill, but the cutter will be most efficient when used with a portable drill in a drill stand or when chucked in a regular drill press.

Smoothing, Shaping, Finishing. No matter how carefully you saw wood, you'll find that the edge can use additional attention before the part is acceptable for assembly. Sometimes, just sanding will do the job, but more often a pass or two with a hand plane should be the preliminary step **(Figure 55).** A plane can be used simply to remove material—for example, to reduce a board's width to the required size. But it best serves its purpose when it does a finishing chore. The cutter is set to produce a shaving thin enough almost to see through.

There are *jack* planes, *fore* planes, *jointer* planes, and others, but the one that is most suitable for general woodworking—or, at least, the one that makes sense to start with—is the *smooth* plane **(Figure 56).** This is the

Fig. 55. The hand plane can be used to remove a lot of material but it's essentially a finishing tool—set to remove ultrathin shavings.

smallest member of the *bench plane* family, usually running about 10 inches long and with a cutting blade about 2 inches wide. The plane's size and weight make it convenient to handle, without reducing its efficiency. Chances are that no matter how many hand planes you add to a collection, you'll never consider the smooth plane obsolete.

The *block plane* **(Figure 57)** is a slightly larger than palm-size tool that is especially good for smoothing end grain and plywood edges. Its blade is set at a more acute angle than that of a bench plane, and the bevel on the blade

Fig. 56. A *smoothing* plane about 10 inches long and with a 2-inch-wide blade is useful as a general-purpose tool.

Fig. 57. The *block* plane is slightly larger than palm-size. It does a good job on end grain and plywood.

Fig. 58. Back up the work with a scrap block when planing end grain. The scrap, instead of the work, will take the feathering and splintering that will occur at the end of the pass.

Fig. 59. The block plane is handy for jobs like this—reducing a dowel for a precise fit.

faces up instead of down. On some jobs, waste made by the tool will resemble sawdust more than shavings.

Any plane, when used across the edge of stock, will cause some splintering at the end of the pass. To prevent this, work as shown in **Figure 58.** The clamped-in-place scrap block splinters instead of the work.

The block plane is useful for chamfering or beveling whether you are working with or across the grain, and can be used delicately enough for jobs such as the one shown in **Figure 59**—reducing a dowel, or any cylinder, just enough to size it for a particular hole.

There are *files* and there are *rasps,* the latter **(Figure 60)** suitable for shaping wood. The basic difference between files and rasps is in the tooth arrangement. Files have continuous, comparatively small teeth that can easily be clogged by wood. When a file is used for woodworking, it should have what is called a "bastard cut," and it should be at least 10 inches long. (Note: File cuts indicate spacing of teeth and are classified as *course, bastard, second,* and *smooth.*)

Fig. 60. Some conventional files can be used to shape wood, but *rasps* like these are much better. Tooth design lets them cut fast and with minimum clogging.

The teeth on a rasp are large, individually cut, and spaced so they can be used on soft material with minimum clogging. Of all the file and rasp shapes—*flat, round, three-square,* and so on—the one called *half-round* will be most functional. In cross-section, the file is shaped like the segment of a circle: one side flat, the other convex. The flat side can be used on flat edges and surfaces and on convex shapes; the half-round side does a good job shaping concave forms **(Figure 61).**

The tangs on files and rasps are sharp enough to injure you; they must never be used without a suitable handle. Grasp the free end of the file carefully. You can scrape fingers if the file moves and your hand doesn't. Wear a glove if you wish, but not a floppy one. Wearing any kind of loose apparel that can snag is poor shop practice. Consider files and rasps as shapers, not finishers. They leave a texture that requires further attention.

Fig. 61. A half-round cross section is handy on a rasp— the flat side can be used on contours and the half-round side on concave forms.

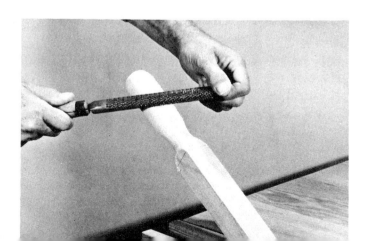

Fig. 62. Formers like these Surform tools are handy. They cut fast, don't clog, and come in sizes and shapes to fit most kinds of work.

Formers, like the Surform tools shown in **Figure 62,** are fine wood shapers. If you've ever used a cheese grater, you'll know how these tools work —the tooth designs and cutting actions are very similar.

The blades of the formers are tool steel. The hundreds of teeth are razor-sharp, and each has a generous "waste route" so clogging is practically nonexistant. As you work, the shavings accumulate inside the tool **(Figure 63)** or fall away from the work area. To clear a tool, simply invert it and tap it gently on a bench-top. The tools can be used cross-grain, but, as with hand planes, results are smoothest when you stroke with the grain of the wood.

The item shown in **Figure 64** is of the Surform family but is designed for use in a portable electric drill or drill press. It does a fast job of preliminary smoothing of regular or irregular curves and of circular, inside cutouts.

Fig. 63. The Surform tools cut on the forward stroke. Shavings will be light or heavy depending on the pressure you apply.

Fig. 64. This type of Surform tool is designed for power drills on inside or outside curves.

Sandpaper is the ultimate finishing tool. Neglect this phase of woodworking and you downgrade all previous effort. This applies to all projects, not just for the sake of appearance but also, in the case of toys, for safe use. Being fastidious with sanding, especially on edges and corners, is the way to avoid splinters. To make a point—any toy in use should be frequently checked to be sure that no damage has occurred that can result in splinters. Such areas should be sanded back smooth.

A good deal of sanding can be done simply by wrapping sandpaper around a block of wood that you can easily grip. This tool can be used to smooth surfaces, edges, round corners, and so on. For *soft* sanding you can cement a piece of indoor-outdoor carpeting, or something similar, to the block of wood **(Figure 65)**. This makes the tool more suitable for smoothing contours, dowels, cylinders **(Figure 66),** etc. It can even be used on those dowels and cylinders to take them down a smidgen for a more precise fit.

Fig. 65. To make a *soft* sanding block, cement a piece of indoor-outdoor carpeting (or something similar) to a block of wood.

Fig. 66. Soft sanding is good for many jobs but especially useful for smoothing contours and round parts. The sandpaper can be held in place with tape, or you can use thumb tacks.

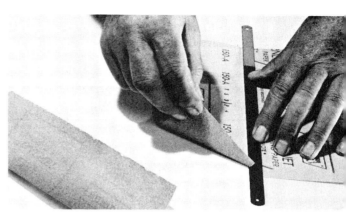

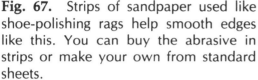

Fig. 67. Strips of sandpaper used like shoe-polishing rags help smooth edges like this. You can buy the abrasive in strips or make your own from standard sheets.

Fig. 68. This is a good way to cut sandpaper. Hold a hacksaw blade firmly down on the paper, and then pull up the paper against the blade's serrated edge.

An efficient way to smooth contours, rounded edges, and the like is shown in **Figure 67:** A strip of sandpaper is gripped and run back and forth like a shoe-polishing rag. You can buy sandpaper in strips, or you can make your own abrasive ribbons from standard sheets. The sheets can be cut with shears, or you can size pieces as shown in **Figure 68.** Hold a hacksaw blade firmly down on the paper; then pull up against the blade's serrated edge.

If you work with power sanders, remember that the *belt sander* is generally used to remove a lot of material quickly. The fine finishing is best done with a *pad sander.*

There are many types and grades of sandpaper, generally classified as *fine, medium,* and *coarse.* The general rule is to work through progressively finer grits of sandpaper until you are satisfied with the smoothness of the wood. But you should judge what grit to start with by the original condition of the wood. It's wrong to automatically reach for coarse paper when the wood is smooth enough to work with only a fine-grit paper.

You can often extend the life of sandpaper if you take this point of view: A worn *coarse* paper might serve for a while longer as *medium* grade; used *medium* paper can often do further duty as a *fine* grade.

Identification of Abrasive Grits			Choose from the categories in relation to the condition of the wood. Some jobs can be done by working with the "fine" category only.
By Name	By Grit No.	By Grade No.	General Use
Very fine	400 360 320 280 240 220	10/0 9/0 8/0 7/0 6/0	For polishing and smoothing between finishing coats and for smoothing the final coat; use after applications of stain, shellac, sealers; also for super-fine finish on raw wood.
Fine	180 150 120	5/0 4/0 3/0	For final smoothing before the application of stains or sealers.
Medium	100 80 60	2/0 1/0 1/2	Intermediate smoothing; to prepare wood for fine sanding; remove any remaining roughness.
Coarse	50 40 36	1 $1\frac{1}{2}$ 2	For initial sanding when necessary; to prepare wood for medium and fine work.
Very coarse	30 24 20 16	$2\frac{1}{2}$ 3 $3\frac{1}{2}$ 4	For very rough work only; may be used on unplaned wood; often used in place of a file to round edges.

Fig. 69. A guide to abrasives.

The charts in **Figures 69** and **70** provide information on abrasive types and grits and make suggestions for correct use.

Basic Facts about Various Abrasives

Type	Super fine	Extra fine	Very fine	Fine	Medium	Coarse	Very coarse	Generally Available in	Wood	Metal	Suggested Applications
				Grits					Use on		
Flint paper			X	X	X	X	X	9 x 10" sheets 4½ x 5" packets	X		Rough work and finishing chores; lacks toughness and durability.
Garnet paper			220 A	120 C	80 D	50 D	30 D	9 x 11" sheets	X		Excellent general abrasive for all woodworking projects.
Aluminum oxide paper			220 A	120 C	80 D	50 D	30 D	9 x 11" sheets	X	X	Good for hardwoods, metals, plastics and other materials; long lasting.
Aluminum oxide cloth			120	80	50	30		in belt form for electric sanders	X	X	Cloth-backed belts are very strong and are a first choice for power-tool sanding.
Silicon carbide waterproof paper	400 A	320 A	220 A					9 x 11" sheets	X	X	Very good for wet sanding after primer coats and between finish coats; can be used with oil and similar lubricants or water.

Note: Letter designation following the grit number indicates the degree of flexibility of the backing: A indicates a thin, soft backing; C and D indicate progressively stiffer and tougher backing.

Fig. 70. The different types of abrasive grits.

Clamps and Glue. It is often said that a woodworking shop can't have too many clamps. It's ideal to have a vast assortment; but the scope of your projects should influence what you invest in. For example, you may never make a project that requires the use of a six-foot bar clamp. More-ordinary clamps make better sense, at least to start with.

C-clamps are so useful for general shop work that several sizes are often included in lists of basic tools. Maximum openings of C-clamps—which indicate the thickness of parts they can grip—range from as little as $\frac{5}{8}$ inch to as much as 18 inches. The smallest ones on up to about 4 or 5 inches are very useful. Another consideration is the depth of the throat. On small standard C-clamps, the throat depth relates to the opening. For example, a $\frac{5}{8}$-inch clamp has a $\frac{7}{8}$-inch throat; a $1\frac{1}{2}$-inch clamp has a 2- or a 3-inch throat. There are also deep-throat C-clamps; for example, a $2\frac{1}{2}$-inch clamp with a 6-inch throat. Deep throats allow you to apply pressure farther in from the edges of stock.

Always use a piece of scrap between the clamp's bearing points and the work **(Figure 71)**. This prevents the clamp from marring the work, and it also spreads the clamp pressure over a wider area.

Spring clamps **(Figure 72)**, which provide you with powerful, tireless fingers, open up to 4 inches. The overall size of the tool and its gripping

Fig. 71. Use protective pads under the jaws of clamps to prevent mars like the one indicated by the arrow.

Fig. 72. Spring clamps are available in many sizes. Some have protective covers over jaws and handles so they're easier to grip and won't mar the work.

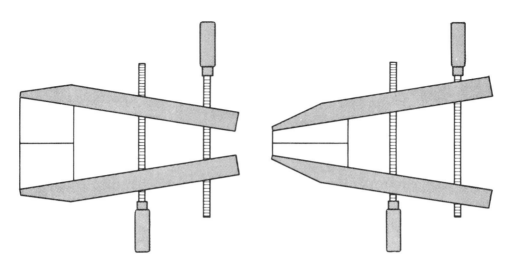

Fig. 73. These are *standard handscrews*—the jaws can be adjusted at an angle. Jaws on nonadjustable types will always remain parallel.

power increase with the maximum opening. The spring on larger ones is so strong, you need two hands to spread the jaws. The pressure applied by the clamp is always at the end of the jaws, so you can pinpoint the grip at any place within the tool's reach.

Spring clamps can be used to hold glued assemblies (as long as the spring pressure is adequate for the job on hand) and for grasping and holding parts you are working on. For example, it can hold several pieces together while you drill through the lot. Some spring clamps have jaws specially designed to grip round objects like dowels or tubing.

Handscrews (**Figure 73**) rate high among woodworkers because they easily adjust to apply parallel pressure over broad areas of the work without marring surfaces. Also, *standard* handscrews have jaws that can be adjusted at an angle; they can be used to hold assemblies of parts that have an angular configuration.

Like most clamps, handscrews come in different sizes. There are three factors to consider: the maximum opening between the jaws, the overall length of the jaws, and the *reach,* which means the grip area. Sizes range

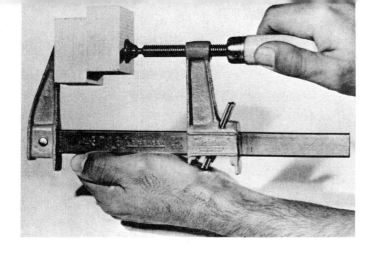

Fig. 74. This is an example of a sliding head bar clamp. Because the head is movable, the clamp can be used to grip any length up to its maximum opening.

from a 2-inch jaw opening with an overall jaw length of 4 inches and a reach of 2 inches, all the way up to a 17-inch jaw opening with a 24-inch jaw length and a reach of 12 inches.

Figure 74 shows an example of a *sliding head bar clamp.* These are available with maximum openings from 6 to more than 72 inches. Generally, you should consider the maximum opening, not the minimum. Because the head slides on the bar, the clamp with the longest opening can be used to grip the thinnest assemblies.

If the scope of your work calls for extra-long clamps, you can use *clamp fixtures* **(Figure 75).** The advantage with these is that with a few sets of fixtures you can make any number of different-length bar clamps merely

Fig. 75. A pipe clamp fixture mounted on black pipe. With a few sets of fixtures and an assortment of pipe, you'll have clamps of whatever length you need.

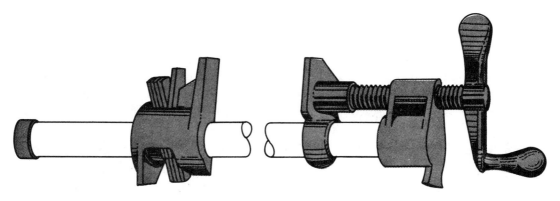

Fig. 76. The traditional woodworker's vise is an integral part of the workbench. The top edges of the vise's jaws are flush with the surface of the bench.

by mounting the fixtures onto various lengths of black pipe. The fixtures are available for mounting on $\frac{1}{2}$- and $\frac{3}{4}$-inch pipe so you can have light-duty or heavy-duty "bar" clamps of any length you wish.

A vise is used primarily to steady stock while you work. The traditional *woodworker's vise* **(Figure 76)** is built into the edge of a workbench with its jaws flush with the bench-top. It has replaceable jaws, usually of wood to avoid marring the work. There are different vise sizes and some variables in design. For example, some vises have a retractable stop, called a dog, in the top edge of the front jaw. When the dog is raised, the vise can be used to apply pressure to work that is backed up by a stop on the top of the bench. It's a way to grip pieces that are wider or longer than the vise's maximum opening.

The example in **Figure 77** is also a woodworker's vise, but is designed for attachment to any surface not more than $2\frac{1}{4}$ inches thick. Thus it can be used on a workbench, a table—even outdoors on a piece of thick plywood that spans a couple of sawhorses. The jaws of this unit are faced with tempered hardboard. They can be replaced, when necessary, with similar material or with wood.

There are many types of glues available for woodworking. When wisely selected and correctly used, the adhesive will form a bond that will hold

Fig. 77. This is also a woodworker's vise, but it can be secured anywhere. The jaw faces, which can be hardboard or wood, are replaceable.

even when surrounding areas fail. Some types of wood are more porous than others, but all are more absorbent at end grain than along edges or on surfaces. It's a good idea, on end grain, first to apply a thinned coat of glue as a sealer. After this soaks in and dries, apply the full-strength bonding coat. You can tell just by looking whether the surface has a uniform coat.

Much of the glue we use today is squeezed out of plastic bottles. This is convenient but often tempts workers to lay the glue in a wavy bead. It's better, after the bead is down, to spread the glue uniformly with a small, stiff brush.

Using too much glue is unnecessary and wasteful, but don't be miserly. The amount of glue that oozes out when parts are put together should be minimal. Remove the excess immediately with a knife or similar tool. Then wipe the area with a damp, lint-free cloth. Glue can act as a sealer to prevent stain or other finishes from penetrating.

The characteristics and uses of most common wood glues are given in **Figure 78.** You should also carefully read the manufacturer's instructions that are printed on the container's label. The label will be specific only for that product and will also tell you of any safety precautions you should follow.

Nuts and Bolts and Washers. These are usually considered heavy-duty fasteners, yet the types that are shown in **Figure 79** do come in sizes that are usable on small projects. Unlike screws, bolts do not thread into wood

Fig. 78. Glues for the woodworker and their uses.

Most Common Wood Glues

Type	Preparation	Clamping Time		Best Temperature °Fahrenheit	Moisture Resistance	Waterproof	Remarks
		Softwood	Hardwood				
Animal liquid hide	Ready to use	3–4 hours	2 hours	70 degrees or over; warm the glue if the room is cold.	Good	No	Good choice for general furniture work but not for outdoor projects. Provides some strength even when joints are poorly fitted. Will resist heat and mold, and is easy to use.
Powdered casein	Mix with water.	3–4 hours	2 hours	Must be above freezing; works best at warmer temperature	Good	No	Especially good for oily woods like yew, teak, lemon, but it will stain woods like redwood. Works fairly well as a joint filler. Okay for general woodworking but do not use on outdoor projects.
Polyvinyl white glue	Ready to use	1½–2 hours	1 hour	60 degree minimum	Good	No	This is a very good all-around glue. It's quick-setting, easy to use, and does not require maximum clamping. Do not use on outdoor projects.
Plastic powdered resin	Mix with water.	16 hours	16 hours	70 degree minimum	High	No	Best for wood projects that will be exposed to considerable moisture and joints that are close fitting and clamped tightly. Not good for oily woods.
Resorcinal	2-part mix; follow directions on container.	16 hours	16 hours	70 degree minimum		Yes	This is the glue to use for outdoor projects, boats, wooden water containers. It is also excellent for joints that are poorly fitted, but do not use when temperature is below 70° F.
Urea resin	2-part mix; follow directions on container.	Requires only seconds with high frequency heat		70 degree minimum	High	No	This is not a typical home workshop adhesive. It works best when moisture content of wood is minimal.
Contact cement	Ready to use	Bonds on contact; no clamping required		70 degree minimum	High	No	Not used for general woodworking. Use for bonding thin materials such as veneers, laminates, plastics and so forth. But remember that parts can't be shifted after contact is made. Read directions carefully.
Epoxy cement	2-part mix	Amount of clamping depends on product but will set faster with heat. Some require none; read directions on the package.				Yes	This is not a general woodworking adhesive, but it is good for bonding dissimilar materials. Some types can be used to fill holes. Use carefully. Read directions on the package.

Fig. 79. Specifications for bolts, types of nuts, washers, and carriage bolts.

MACHINE BOLTS		
Diameter in inches	*Length in inches*	
$\frac{1}{4}$	$\frac{1}{2}$ to 8	hex head
$\frac{5}{16}$	$\frac{1}{2}$ to 10	
$\frac{3}{8}$	$\frac{3}{4}$ to 12	
$\frac{7}{16}$	1 to 12	countersunk head oval or button head
$\frac{1}{2}$	1 to 25	

STOVE BOLTS	
Diameter in inches	*Length in inches*
$\frac{1}{8} - \frac{5}{32}$	$\frac{3}{8}$ to 2
$\frac{3}{16}$	$\frac{3}{8}$ to 6
$\frac{1}{4}$	$\frac{1}{2}$ to 6
$\frac{5}{16} - \frac{3}{8}$	$\frac{3}{4}$ to 6
$\frac{1}{2}$	1 to 4

button head   countersunk head   truss head

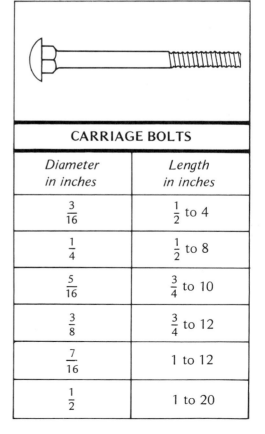

CARRIAGE BOLTS	
Diameter in inches	*Length in inches*
$\frac{3}{16}$	$\frac{1}{2}$ to 4
$\frac{1}{4}$	$\frac{1}{2}$ to 8
$\frac{5}{16}$	$\frac{3}{4}$ to 10
$\frac{3}{8}$	$\frac{3}{4}$ to 12
$\frac{7}{16}$	1 to 12
$\frac{1}{2}$	1 to 20

NUTS

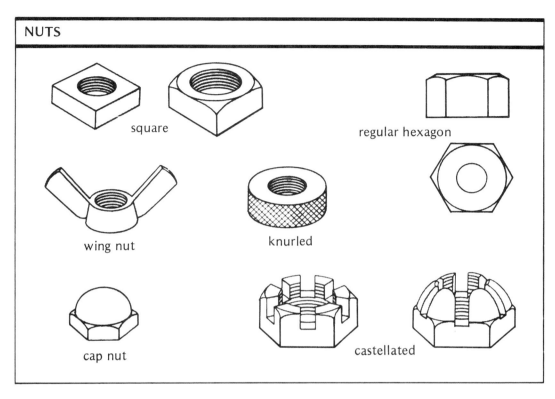

square

regular hexagon

wing nut

knurled

cap nut

castellated

WASHERS

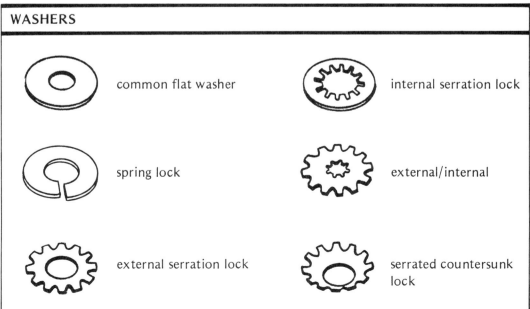

common flat washer

internal serration lock

spring lock

external/internal

external serration lock

serrated countersunk lock

but pass through full-size holes. Because they are easy to remove, bolts are often chosen for projects, like outdoor furniture, that you might want to break down for storage.

A useful, not unattractive, fastener for woodworking is the *carriage bolt,* which is available with either a round or an oval head. This bolt has a square shoulder directly under the head that bites into the wood, preventing the bolt from turning when you tighten the nut. The carriage bolt takes a washer only under the nut. Other types, unless they have countersunk heads, can be used with washers under both head and nut.

Using Throw-Aways.   **Figures 80** and **81** show typical items we usually throw away but which can serve, sometimes with modification, as project components. For example, some caps from fancy bottles of perfume or cologne are nicely shaped for use as a stack on a toy locomotive. Others seem to have been specially designed to serve as a horn button on a car or as ready-to-glue-on headlights. Items like the reels of adding-machine

Fig. 80. Caps from fancy perfume and cologne bottles and similar containers can be ready-made components of toys, such as stacks for locomotives and horn buttons for cars.

Fig. 81. Other recyclable items are shown here. Some can be used as is; others can be altered to serve as bushings, spacers, etc.

tapes can serve as short dowels, bushings, or spacers. Some wood caps after being plugged are attractive ready-made wheels.

Other items that can be recycled include mailing tubes, jar covers, the handles of discarded brooms, coat hangers (when you need a piece of wire), the round containers that salt and some cereals are packed in, and so on. It's a question of seeing the items as usable material.

Copying Patterns. Many of the patterns in the book, especially the silhouette forms in the toys section, can be reproduced by using the enlarging-by-squares method **(Figure 82)**. The system is this: Assume the drawing in the book is done on graph paper. You draw a graph with squares sized as the drawing suggests and then mark points where the pattern crosses lines. Then it's a matter of connecting the points.

Once the pattern is drawn, you can transfer it to the wood by using carbon paper. As an alternative you can cement the pattern directly to the wood. Or, if you wish to keep the design for future use, use the pattern to make a permanent template of thin plywood or hardboard. Of course, you can also draw the enlarging graph (with very light lines) directly onto the wood. You can also take a photograph of the book drawing and then enlarge it in the darkroom.

The enlarging-by-squares method can also be used in reverse. For example, if you happen onto an illustration in a magazine that you'd like to reproduce but that is too large for your purposes, put a graph over the illustration and transfer the pattern to a sheet of paper with squares of smaller size.

Finishing. As we said earlier, children don't object to the natural look of wood **(Figure 83)**. A very careful sanding job followed by a coat or two of nontoxic sealer or clear finish makes a presentable finale. For decorative touches, you can work with materials like self-adhesive stars, felt, tapes, letters, and numbers—all of which are available in a stationery store. Of course, work with colors if you prefer. It's important to choose nontoxic

Fig. 82. This illustrates how to enlarge or reduce a drawing when transferring it from a pattern to the work. The procedure is known as enlarging by squares.

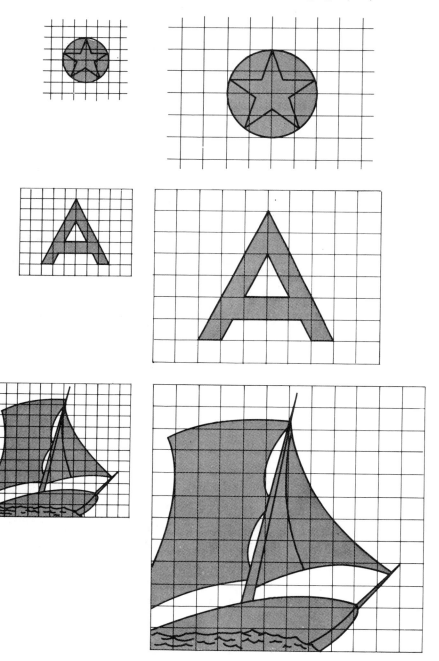

Fig. 83. Children don't seem to mind that the toy projects have a natural wood finish. You can add decorative details by working with some of the self-adhesive materials suggested in the text.

paints, which isn't difficult to do these days since lead and other poison bases have been outlawed.

Finishes for other types of projects are also available in nontoxic form. These include polyurethanes that can serve as primers, sealers, or finishes in themselves **(Figure 84)**. Some require brush applications; others can simply be wiped on with a cloth. Instructions on the container will list the correct methods of application.

Polyurethanes are not recommended for use on projects such as cutting boards. Polyurethane flakes may present a health hazard, and marks from knife blades will mar the finish.

There is a special finish called "Salad Bowl Finish" that is a good choice for final touches on cutting boards, salad bowls, and the like. Because of its nontoxic formulation, it's also a good finish for toys and other projects used by children.

Fig. 84. Modern polyurethane materials that are nontoxic can be used on toys and other projects. Some are applied with a brush, others with a cloth. Follow the instructions on the container.

Another way to finish projects that come into contact with food is to use mineral oil. Apply a generous amount and allow it to soak in for 30 minutes or so. Then wipe off the excess. You can renew the finish when necessary simply by applying more of the oil. Don't use cooking oils for this purpose —they can turn rancid.

II.
MAINLY
FOR
KIDS:

TOYS

WHEELS
AND AXLES

The easiest way to make small wheels is to slice them from dowels. Typically, dowels are made of maple or birch, come in 3- or 4-foot lengths, and range in diameters from $\frac{1}{8}$ inch up to more than 1 inch. Larger diameters and longer lengths are available as "rounds." The term includes a variety of molding products such as *half rounds* and *quarter rounds, closet rods* or "poles," and *hand rails* which are shown in **Figure 1.** Closet-rod diameters are usually about $1\frac{5}{8}$ or $1\frac{3}{4}$ inches. The hand rail is shown because the flat it has makes it easy to attach the cylinder to a flat surface; for, say, the boiler on a toy locomotive.

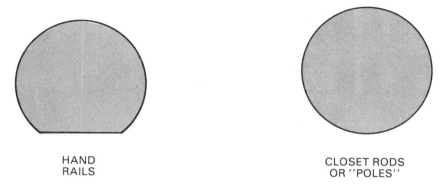

HAND
RAILS

CLOSET RODS
OR "POLES"

Fig. 1. "Rounds" are available as closet rods or poles, or as hand rails. Rails have a "flat" which makes the part suitable for attachment to a flat surface.

Figure 2 shows how dowels can be sliced on a table saw. It is never a good or safe practice to use the rip fence as a stop to gauge the thickness of the cutoff. The cutoff piece might be captured between the fence and saw blade and could be thrown back or up at the operator, or the wood may bind the blade. The fence is used only as a holder for the jig, which serves as a stop. The distance from the front edge of the jig—which is clamped to the rip fence well forward of the saw blade—to the saw blade determines the

Fig. 2. Always use a stop—not the rip fence—to determine the thickness of cutoffs. Hold the work firmly against the stop and stand clear of the cutting path.

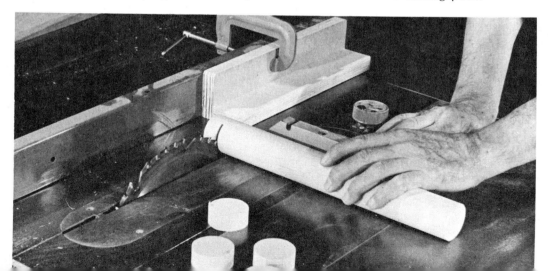

thickness of the cutoff. The setup provides a lot of room between rip fence and blade, so the cutoff can't be trapped.

Because the dowel pieces are round, after they are cut off they can still roll back toward you, but not with any force. Still, it's always a good idea to stand out of line of the saw blade. Scrap pieces of wood are often used as stops in this application, but you will find it more convenient to make the special jig **(Figure 3)** which you can keep on hand as an accessory.

Fig. 3.   Here is a cut-off gauge, shown in the previous photo, that you can make and keep as an accessory. Glue and nail the parts together. Sand the wood smooth, round off corners, and apply a coat of sealer.

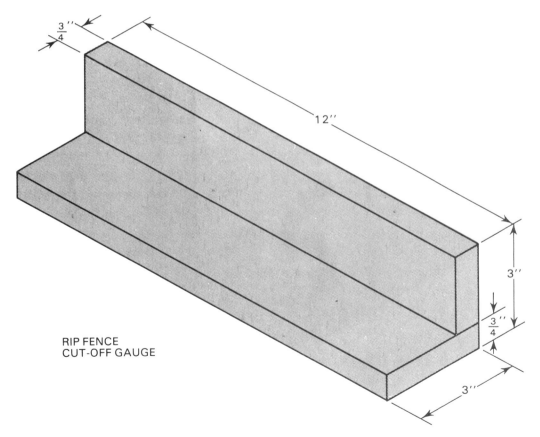

RIP FENCE
CUT-OFF GAUGE

Dowels and rounds can be cut freehand with a hand saw, but an accurate job will demand great care. A better way is to make the cutoff box shown in **Figure 4.** This is a smaller version of the miter box we have already talked about, but it has a single guide kerf and its size is more suitable for the materials you will be cutting. A more sophisticated version of the cutoff box is shown in **Figure 5.** Here the base of the project has a V-channel so that rounds can be seated more securely. Either unit can be used with a conventional hand saw, but the cut edges will be easier to smooth if you work with a backsaw.

To locate the center of the cut-off dowel—so you can drill them for axles

Fig. 4.   The cut-off box resembles a miter box, but has a single guide-kerf and is sized to be more suitable for dowels and other cylinders.

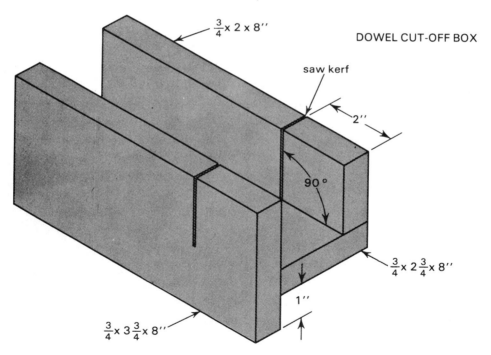

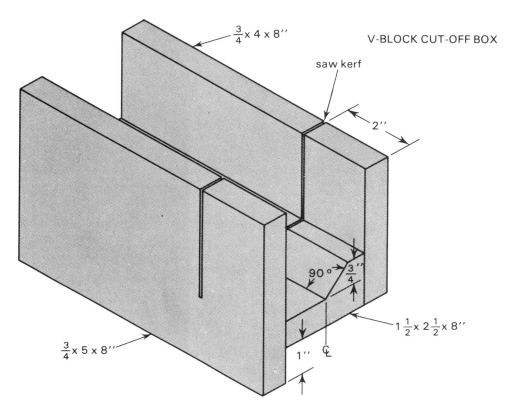

Fig. 5. This version of cut-off box has a V-shape channel in the base to hold round forms more securely.

—you can use a commercial center finder, or make one of the two styles shown in **Figure 6.** You may find the alternative design easier to build since it only calls for straight cuts. Either project serves the purpose and is used as follows: Place the round in the V and mark a diameter along the centered edge of the guide. Turn the part about 90 degrees and mark a second diameter. The center of the round will be where the lines intersect.

The center finder isn't limited to marking wheel centers. It can also be used for other jobs, such as marking mounting points on the ends of stock that will be turned in a lathe.

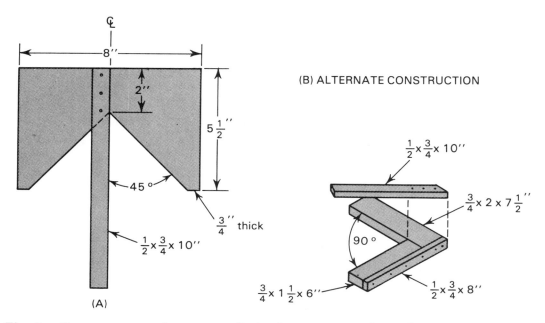

Fig. 6. Two ways to make a center finder for sawing. Each can be used to mark the center of round or square stock.

DRILLING AXLE HOLES

Wheels can be individually marked and drilled, but this practice poses the possibility of error. That can be a nuisance if you are producing in quantity. A better strategy is to make the center-drilling jig shown in **Figure 7.** It can be used on a drill press or on a portable drill stand.

The jig works as follows: Use the center finder to mark the center location of one piece. Place the piece in the V of the jig, and then clamp the jig in place so that the center mark of the workpiece will be exactly under the drill bit. Then you can drill through as many parts as you wish without further layout. It's a good idea to use this jig to drill pilot holes. Later, the holes can be enlarged to whatever size is needed.

Construction details of the jig are shown in **Figure 8.** To make the T-slot, first form the $\frac{3}{16} \times \frac{5}{8}$-inch dado clear across the base of the jig. Then cut the $\frac{1}{4}$-inch-wide slot. The guides form a V whose point should be exactly

Fig. 7. The center-drilling jig makes it easy to accurately drill center holes in one or more pieces. Layout is done only on first piece, the one that is used to position the jig on the drill table.

Fig. 8. Construction details of the center-drilling jig. The text explains how the T-slot is formed.

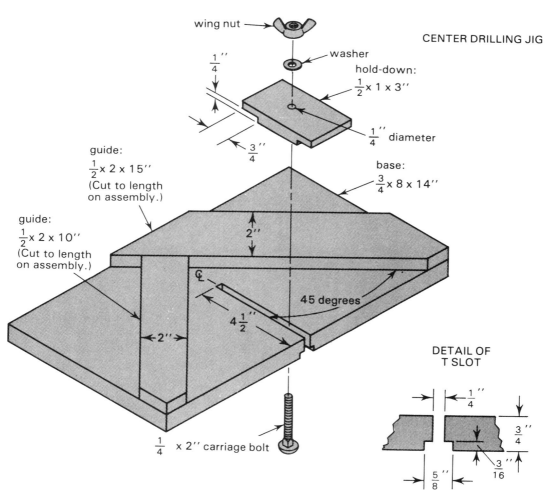

CENTER DRILLING JIG

wing nut

washer

hold-down:
$\frac{1}{2}$ x 1 x 3''

$\frac{1}{4}$''

$\frac{3}{4}$

$\frac{1}{4}$'' diameter

guide:
$\frac{1}{2}$ x 2 x 15''
(Cut to length on assembly.)

base:
$\frac{3}{4}$ x 8 x 14''

guide:
$\frac{1}{2}$ x 2 x 10''
(Cut to length on assembly.)

2''

C L

4 $\frac{1}{2}$''

45 degrees

2''

$\frac{1}{4}$ x 2'' carriage bolt

DETAIL OF T SLOT

$\frac{1}{4}$''

$\frac{3}{4}$''

$\frac{3}{16}$''

$\frac{5}{8}$''

Fig. 9. The center-drilling jig can also be used to drill center holes in square pieces. The procedure does not change.

on the centerline of the T-slot. The hold-down makes sense since it's often inconvenient, sometimes unsafe, to hand-hold small parts. As shown in **Figure 9,** the jig can also be used to drill center holes in square pieces.

LARGE WHEELS

Several types of tools can be used to form wheels with larger diameters than you can get from the largest ready-made rounds or dowels. *Hole saws* are available as individual units that mount on a universal mandrel. Each saw cuts a particular size disc, sizes can exceed 4 inches.

Another type of hole saw is shown in **Figure 10.** Because it comes with various blades, the one tool can be used to form discs that range in size from

Fig. 10. This type of hole saw comes with various blades—so the tool is usable for different size discs. All the blades mount on the single hub.

Fig. 11. Both the work and the back-up block should be securely clamped. The tool has a drill-pilot that bores a center or axle hole as it cuts the disc.

$1-2\frac{1}{2}$ inches. The saw is available with blade lengths that can penetrate $\frac{3}{4}$-inch stock, or with extra-long blades that can cut 2 inches deep.

Tools like this can be used in a portable drill or in a drill press **(Figure 11)**. With either tool, back up the work with scrap so the hole will be clean where the saw breaks through. Also, be sure that the work and the back-up block are securely clamped. One advantage of these saws is that they have a center drill. Thus, an exactly centered axle hole is formed as you cut the disc.

The tools shown in **Figure 12** are called *fly cutters* or *circle cutters.* They come in several sizes. "Small" ones can typically cut circles from about $1\frac{1}{8}$ inches up to better than 5 inches; "large" ones range from $1\frac{3}{4}$ inches to better than 8 inches. Tools like these require that you first drill a center hole for the pilot, and the cutters *must* be used in a drill press **(Figure 13)** at very slow speeds. Both the work and a back-up block should be securely clamped, and the feed pressure (the amount you pull on the drill press handle) should be light. Keep hands well away from the cutting area, since even at a slow speed the cutter will be a blur.

The fly cutter can be used to shape decorative, concentric grooves **(Figure 14)**. Simply cut smaller, limited-depth circles before you cut through for the disc. If you wish, you can grind a special point on a cutter for this kind of work. For example, a half-round shape that will produce cove-shaped grooves. You can also form decorative grooves with the hole saws. Just make shallow grooves with a number of smaller hole saws before you use the one that cuts through the material.

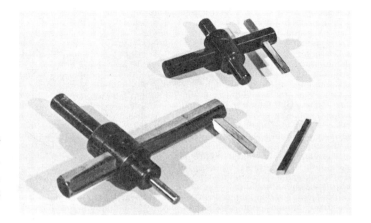

Fig. 12. Two sizes of fly cutters: like the hole saws, they are meant to cut holes, but they also cut out discs which make great wheels.

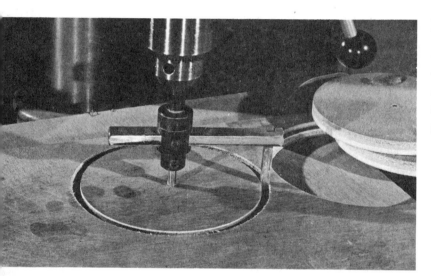

Fig. 13. The fly cutters are used in a drill press, *never* with a portable drill. Keep work and back-up block securely clamped. Use a slow speed and very light feed pressure.

Fig. 14. Forming decorative grooves by making smaller-than-wheel-size, limited-depth cuts. The same thing can be done with hole saws.

OTHER WHEEL-FORMING TECHNIQUES

Figure 15 shows a drill-press pivot-cutting method that can be used to cut circles or grooves of almost any size. Drive a nail through a back-up block, and then clamp the block to the drill table so that the distance from the nail to the cutter (a router bit) equals the radius of the circle. The work is drilled to fit the pivot nail, and then placed in position for cutting. Use a high drill-press speed, and if necessary, make repeat passes to achieve full depth of cut; lower the router bit a little for each rotation of the work. The depth of each cut will depend on the hardness of the wood. In general, a few shallow cuts will produce smoother results than a single, deep one.

The pivot-cutting method can also be used with a portable router. Drill a hole for a small nail at one end of a length of dowel or steel rod. Lock the other end of the rod in one of the holes normally used for the router's edge guide. The distance from the nail to the router bit will be the radius

Fig. 15. This drill-press, pivot technique lets you cut wheel discs of almost any size. Hold the work firmly and rotate it slowly against the router bit's direction of rotation.

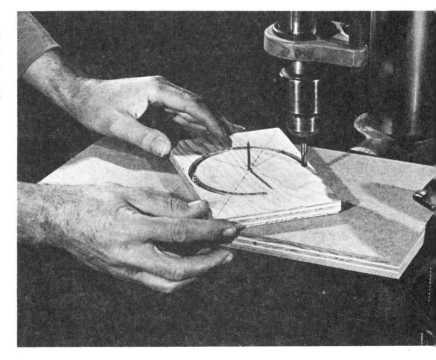

Fig. 16. The pivot-cutting method can also be used with a portable router. The size of the disc is limited only by the size of the material. Thus you can cut table tops as well as wheels for toys.

of the circle. The router is then pivoted about the nail to form a perfect circle **(Figure 16).** Here too, results will be better if you make several passes, deepening the cut each time. Techniques like this are not limited to wheel-making. They can be used to form circular pieces for table tops and the like.

SMOOTHING WHEEL RIMS

Wheel rims can be sanded by hand, but there are methods that will make this chore easier and more accurate. One way is to mount a pair of wheels, or more, on a bolt, and secure them with a nut. Lock the free end of the bolt in the chuck of a portable drill, and secure the drill in a vise. Wrap a piece of sandpaper around a block of wood, and then apply the sandpaper to the turning wheels.

If you want to chamfer the wheel rims or round them off, mount the wheels individually on the bolt. This method can also be used on a drill press.

The jig shown in **Figure 17** allows fast sanding of circular edges with great accuracy. The jig is shown clamped to a disc-sander table, but it is just as usable on a belt sander or even a drill press that is turning a drum sander.

The jig is clamped to the tool's table so that its forward edge clears the abrasive surface. The work is mounted on the dowel/pivot, and the guide bar moved forward until the disc touches the abrasive. Then the guide bar

Fig. 17. The sanding jig for circles is shown here mounted on a disc sander, but it can be used on a belt sander or a drill press fitted with a drum sander as well.

is clamped into place and the work rotated. Make alignment marks on the guide bar and the jig (arrow in **Figure 17**) so duplicate pieces can be accurately reproduced **(Figure 18)**. The dowel/pivot is long enough so that you can mount pairs of $\frac{3}{4}$-inch-thick wheels. If the wheels are thicker, and the capacity of the sanding tool permits it, you can substitute a longer dowel. Of course, you can also simultaneously sand a set of four wheels if wheel thickness, dowel/pivot length, and tool capacity are compatible. It is possible to pivot-sand four $\frac{1}{2}$- or $\frac{3}{4}$-inch-thick wheels. Four wheels that

Fig. 18. The work is mounted on the dowel/post and rotated. Pairs of wheels can be mounted and sanded simultaneously for a perfect match.

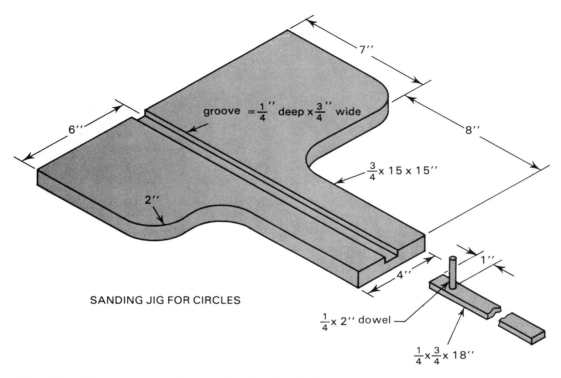

groove $= \frac{1}{4}''$ deep x $\frac{3}{4}''$ wide

7''

6''

8''

$\frac{3}{4}$ x 15 x 15''

2''

1''

4''

SANDING JIG FOR CIRCLES

$\frac{1}{4}$ x 2'' dowel

$\frac{1}{4}$ x $\frac{3}{4}$ x 18''

Fig. 19. How to make the sanding jig for circles.

are $1\frac{1}{2}$ inches thick would present problems. Better do them individually or, at most, in pairs. Construction details of the circular sanding jig are shown in **Figure 19.**

WHEELS FROM READY-MADES

Wheels can be made from items like the curtain rings shown in **Figure 20.** These come in different sizes and are available in wood, metal, and plastic. The wooden ones in the photograph have an outside diameter of

$2\frac{3}{4}$ inches; the metal ones have an outside diameter of $1\frac{1}{2}$ inches. The rings have hangers, but they're not difficult to remove. Hangers on the wooden rings are just screw eyes that you simply unwind; on others the hangers can be removed by filing.

To turn the rings into wheels, cut snug-fitting wood or hardboard discs and press them into place—the rings become "tires" **(Figures 21** and **22).** You can size the discs for a nice fit with a fly cutter. It should require a *little* force to seat the discs, but be careful when working with wooden rings. If the discs are too large the rings will split. Coat the perimeter of the discs with glue before you install them.

Figure 23 is an example of novelty wheels. These were made from tops of fancy bottles of cologne. The tops will usually have threaded inserts of metal or plastic. To remove the metal inserts, bend the top edge with a small screwdriver and use pliers to break the bond that holds the insert. The plastic inserts can simply be broken away, but protect your eyes from flying chips. The final step is to glue a center-drilled wooden plug into the hole.

Fig. 20. Curtain rings provide ready-made materials for wheels. They come in different sizes and are made of wood, plastic, and metal.

Fig. 21. The rings become good-looking wheels when they are filled with discs of wood or hardboard. Size discs for wooden rings carefully so that when you press them into place they won't split the ring.

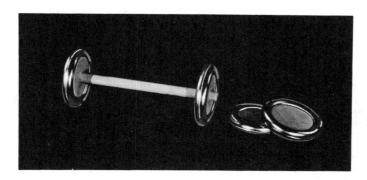

Fig. 22. Plastic or metal rings also make handsome wheels. Such curtain rings have hangers (usually a loop) that must be filed off.

Fig. 23. Novelty wheels were made from the wooden tops from fancy bottles of cologne. The threaded inserts are removed, and the hole is filled with a predrilled wooden plug.

WHEEL RIMS OR "TIRES"

Rims can be added to wooden wheels for a decorative touch, to protect floors or furniture, or to make the wheels more durable. **Figure 24** shows small wheels rimmed with plastic obtained from the canisters that 35mm film is packed in. The idea is to size a dowel or a turned cylinder to make a very tight fit in the canister. Then simply cut the canister into wheel thicknesses. Note that the rim and the outside surface of the wheel can be covered if you utilize the bottom of the canister. Many similar containers can be adapted for wheels of various diameters.

A "soft" rim is shown in **Figure 25.** This is simply a strip of cork that is attached with contact cement or white glue. If you use white glue, coat both the cork and the wheel rim. Use a heavy rubber band to hold the cork until the glue dries.

To make a wooden wheel more durable you can rim it with metal **(Figure 26)**. Metals that work easily include aluminum or various types of flashing —the material used on roofs. Either material can be attached with contact cement or very small nails. If using nails, put two on each side of the joints and two or three more about the wheel's perimeter. Use a file to chamfer the edges of the metal, and then sand the edges smooth with emery paper.

Fig. 24. The plastic rims on these wheels came from 35-mm film canisters. Similar throwaways can serve as rims for wheels of various sizes.

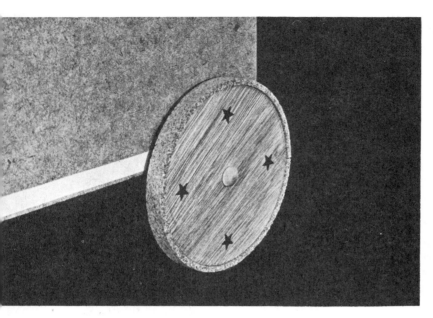

Fig. 25. This wheel is rimmed with cork to prevent marring of floors or furniture. A cork rim will also be quieter than a wooden one. Note the wood button used as a hub and the self-adhesive decorative stars.

Fig. 26. Metal rims make wooden wheels more durable. The metal can be easy-to-form aluminum or flashing, and can be secured with contact cement.

MAKING RIMS AND WOODEN TUBES

Parts like those shown in **Figure 27** are not difficult to make from large rounds or turned cylinders if you work very carefully and use a drilling procedure like the one demonstrated in **Figure 28.**

Fig. 27. Wooden rings and tubes can be made from rounds or lathe-turned cylinders. Don't make the wall thickness of the pieces too thin, or they won't hold up.

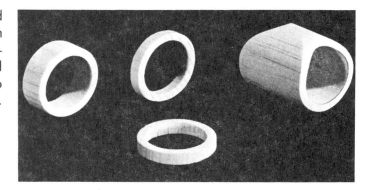

Fig. 28. Here's a way to make a wooden tube, which can be used as is or sliced into rings. This is a fly cutter, but one that removes material much as a conventional hole former does. Caution: Use care to avoid wood breakage here.

The drilling tool being used is a type of fly cutter, but instead of cutting circular grooves, it removes material just like a conventional drill bit. It's very important that the work be held securely and that the drilling pressure be very light. The advantage of the fly cutter is that you can form tubes of various inside diameters. Of course, for small tubes, you can work with conventional drills or spade bits. For rims and short tubes, the job can be done with a hole saw.

You can do some of this work with an electric hand drill, or even with a hand brace, but generally it's recommended that the operation be performed on a drill press.

WHEEL AND AXLE ASSEMBLIES

The four most common wheel assemblies for push or pull toys are shown in **Figure 29.** Sometimes the choice is arbitrary; other times you can opt for a design that provides necessary stability. For example, design A of **Figure 29** will do for a small animal silhouette on wheels. But if the figure is tall, it will be less likely to topple if the wheels are spread by spacers or if it has a base, designs B or C.

Wheels can rotate on the axles, or axles and wheels can turn together **(Figure 30).** One advantage of using dowels as axles is that dowels are generally available a bit oversize. This means that if you want a $\frac{1}{4}$-inch dowel to fit tightly in a wheel or body of a toy, you just drill a $\frac{1}{4}$-inch hole. If the dowels you buy are more precise than usual, you can still work with the dowel-size hole if you use some glue to bond the connection.

If the wheel must turn on the axle or the axle must turn in the body of the toy, drill holes that are just oversize enough to permit the action—$\frac{5}{16}$-inch holes for $\frac{1}{4}$-inch dowels, $\frac{7}{16}$-inch holes for $\frac{3}{8}$-inch dowels, $\frac{9}{16}$-inch holes for $\frac{1}{2}$-inch dowels, and so on.

Wheels that turn on wooden axles are often secured with a short dowel **(Figure 31).** The dowel must fit the hole through the axle tightly and be located so the wheel can't bind. When you drive home a dowel retainer, do

Fig. 29. Here are basic wheel assemblies for pull or push toys. Wider-spread wheels give toys more stability.

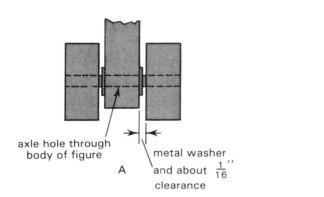

axle hole through
body of figure

A

metal washer
and about $\frac{1}{16}$''
clearance

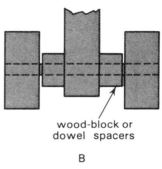

wood-block or
dowel spacers

B

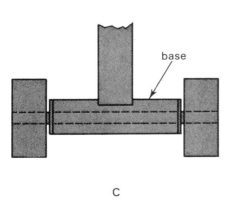

base

C

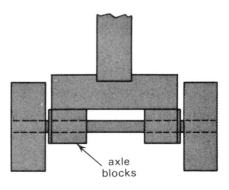

axle
blocks

D

Fig. 30.   This drawing tells what conditions must be met for the wheels to turn independently or to rotate with the axles. It's always a good idea to use a washer (metal or hardboard) between the body and wheels.

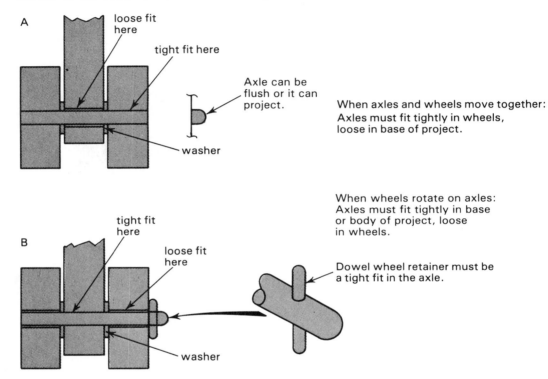

When axles and wheels move together: Axles must fit tightly in wheels, loose in base of project.

When wheels rotate on axles: Axles must fit tightly in base or body of project, loose in wheels.

Fig. 31. Wheels that rotate independently of the axle can be secured with a dowel that passes through the axle. Place the dowel so that the wheel can turn without binding.

it gently to avoid splitting the axle. Chamfering the ends of the retainer will make it easier to insert and will also add to appearance.

WHEEL/AXLE ASSEMBLIES FOR ACTION

One way to make the head, ears, or tail of an animal pull toy nod or waggle is to use an axle that is bent into a U-shape at its center **(Figure 32).** One end of the connecting rod loops around the base of the U, and the other end links to the part that moves. Make the axles from wire that is at least

Fig. 32. This is a popular method for producing action in a toy. The free end of the connecting rod, or drive wire, connects to the part that nods or waggles.

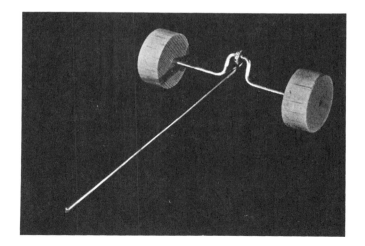

Fig. 33. Don't overdo the depth of the U-shape (dimension B) in the axle. A $\frac{1}{2}$-inch U-depth will result in a 1-inch stroke, and that will produce quite visible action.

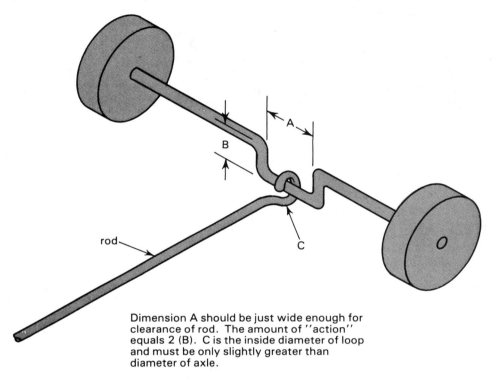

Dimension A should be just wide enough for clearance of rod. The amount of "action" equals 2 (B). C is the inside diameter of loop and must be only slightly greater than diameter of axle.

No. 10 gauge ($\frac{1}{8}$-inch diameter). The connecting rod or drive wire can be of similar material or thinner wire, say No. 16 gauge ($\frac{1}{16}$-inch diameter).

The U-shape can be made with a pair of flat-nose pliers. Grip the length of wire close to its center, and bend the ends so you will have the base of the U. Then use the pliers to grip at the sides of the U and bend the free ends of the wire 90 degrees. Some gentle tapping with a hammer with the wire resting on a piece of hardwood or a metal block will straighten imperfections. It's best to work with a piece of wire that is longer than you need. Then you can be sure that the U will be centered by trimming the ends of the wire.

Form loops on the connecting rod by bending the wire around a piece of steel. Start the loop by gripping the wire against the rod with pliers. Move the pliers as you continue to form the loop. **Figure 33** illustrates some facts that apply to this type of action-axle.

Animal pull toys such as bunnies can be made to hop if you use an off-center axle at either the front or the rear of the toy **(Figure 34).** Don't

Fig. 34. Axles placed off-center will cause animal pull toys to hop. There is a limit to the amount of offset you can use. Too much, and the wheels won't turn.

off center

true center

Fig. 35. An eccentric cam placed on the axle will move the part placed on it up and down.

overdo the offset or the wheels won't turn as the toy is pulled. An offset of about $\frac{1}{4}$ inch will cause an easily noticeable hopping action.

Another way to make a toy hop or have an up-and-down action is to mount a cam on the axle **(Figure 35).** The animal, or whatever, that must move is pivot-mounted at one end. The other end rests on the cam and hops because of the eccentric cam rotation. **Figure 36** shows an important factor

Fig. 36. Situate the eccentric cam so that it won't bind against the surface the wheels are rolling on.

Distance A must be less than distance B.
Axle must fit tight into wheels *and* cam.

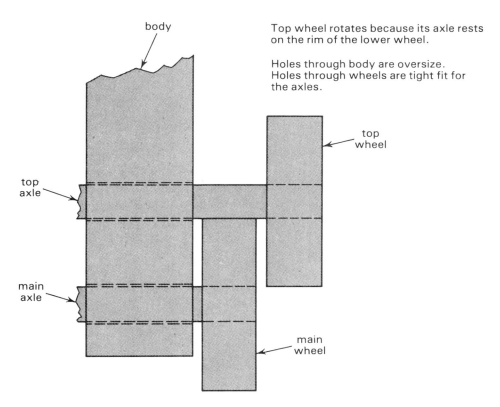

body

Top wheel rotates because its axle rests on the rim of the lower wheel.

Holes through body are oversize. Holes through wheels are tight fit for the axles.

top wheel

top axle

main axle

main wheel

Fig. 37. An auxiliary axle situated to rest on the rim of a main wheel will cause other parts to turn. This is the action that is used on the Pinwheel Toy shown later.

about cam action. You don't want the cam so big that it touches the same plane (or ground) that the wheels roll on.

Wheels can be organized to turn accessory axles and to rotate other parts of the project **(Figure 37).** The idea is to locate the extra axle to rest on the perimeter of the main wheel. All of these action designs are used on some of the projects that will follow.

AT THE END OF THE AXLE

Three ways to finish the ends of wooden axles are shown in **Figure 38.**
Most times, the choice is optional. These ideas apply when wheels and axles

Fig. 38. Three ways to end an axle. These ideas apply mostly to wooden axles.

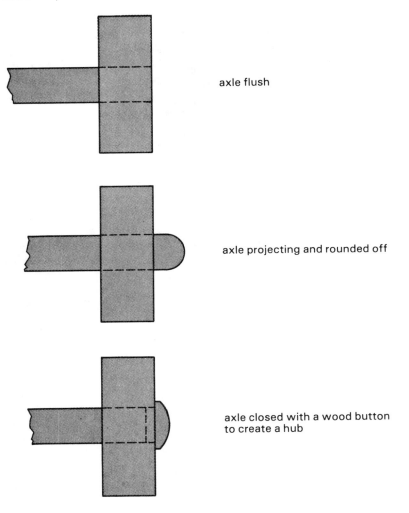

axle flush

axle projecting and rounded off

axle closed with a wood button
to create a hub

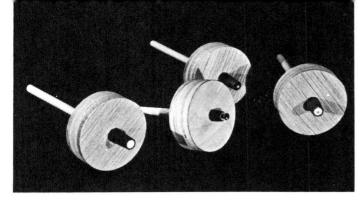

Fig. 39. These axle hubs were made by cutting off the ends of pens that were no longer usable. Similarly, many other throwaways can be recycled.

turn together. When the wheel turns on the axle, the axle must project and a retainer of some sort is used to keep the wheel in place. When the axle is wood, the dowel retainer we talked about can be used. If the axle is metal, you can tap on metal *caps,* which are generally available. Or use *shaft collars,* which lock in place with a set screw. Both items come in various sizes.

Figure 39 shows examples of hubs made from throwaways. These were cut from the ends of used pens, but there are many other items that will serve the same purpose. Choose something that is a reasonably good fit for the axle. Use glue or cement to bond the hub in place.

BASIC PULL TOYS

**Puppy Pull Toy.
Hippo Pull Toy.
Whale of a Pull.
Spotty Dog.
Drag a Dragon.**

The Puppy Pull Toy was painted in a tan tone. Details were done with a black felt-tip pen. Wheels and axles are natural. The spacers are a contrasting color. Scale drawings for similar toys are shown on upcoming pages.

PROJECT 1
PUPPY PULL TOY
Scale: one square = $\frac{1''}{4}$

These projects are typical of pull toys that merely involve cutting silhouettes and then mounting them on wheels. Duplicate the figure by following one of the methods that were suggested on page 61, such as the enlarging-by-squares method. You can cut with a coping saw or saber saw, or on a jigsaw. If you wish, you can use a saber saw or a jigsaw to produce two silhouettes with a single cutting by making a layer or stack of two pieces of $\frac{3}{4}$-inch stock. Of course, the cutting can also be done on a band saw equipped with a narrow blade. Common band saws have a 6-inch depth of cut, which allows the pads to be considerably thicker—a good idea for producing in quantity.

You can work with either lumber or plywood. In either case, be sure that cut edges are sanded smooth and that edges are slightly rounded. Plywood edges will require more attention than lumber. Be sure to fill any voids with wood dough. For a natural finish, apply more sealer to edges than to surfaces. Allow it to soak in, and when dry, repeat the application if necessary.

A good way to prepare plywood edges for paint is as follows: Choose a putty, like Duratite's, which comes as a white powder. You mix the powder with water for use, to control the consistency. Thus you can produce a thin or a thick coating and brush it on the plywood edges. Allow the coating to dry, sand it smooth, and you have a respectable base for paint.

The drawing of Project 1 details the wheel/axle arrangement, and tells what the hole sizes should be. In this case, wheels and axles turn together. The spacers are made from dowel, but you can substitute if you wish.

project 1

Puppy Pull Toy

MATERIALS LIST

Axles = $\frac{1}{4}$" dowel × $4\frac{1}{2}$"
Holes through body *and* spacers = $\frac{5}{16}$"
Holes through wheels = $\frac{1}{4}$"
Body lumber or plywood = $\frac{3}{4}$ × 8 × 10"

Sections cut from plastic or cardboard tubes that have thick walls will serve as well.

Use a length of strong string as the pull, tying it at one end to a small screweye placed in the figure. The free end of the string can simply be knotted, or you can use a wooden bead as a "handle." Wood beads of various sizes are available in craft supply stores, or you can make your own by drilling a hole through a short length of dowel. Place the screweye down low on the figure. The toy will more likely tip over if the pull is high.

PROJECTS 2, 3, 4, and 5

These projects are made by following the same procedures outlined for the Puppy Pull Toy. Each silhouette pattern (see drawings) shows the location of axle holes and suggests wheel sizes. The wheel/axle arrangement can be like the one used on the puppy, or you can substitute one of the ideas that were shown in wheel-and-axle section earlier.

Some of the patterns are whimsical; children seem to enjoy this. Don't feel that artistic realism is a must when you design original forms. Often, you can "draw" with a compass and French curve and similar drafting instruments.

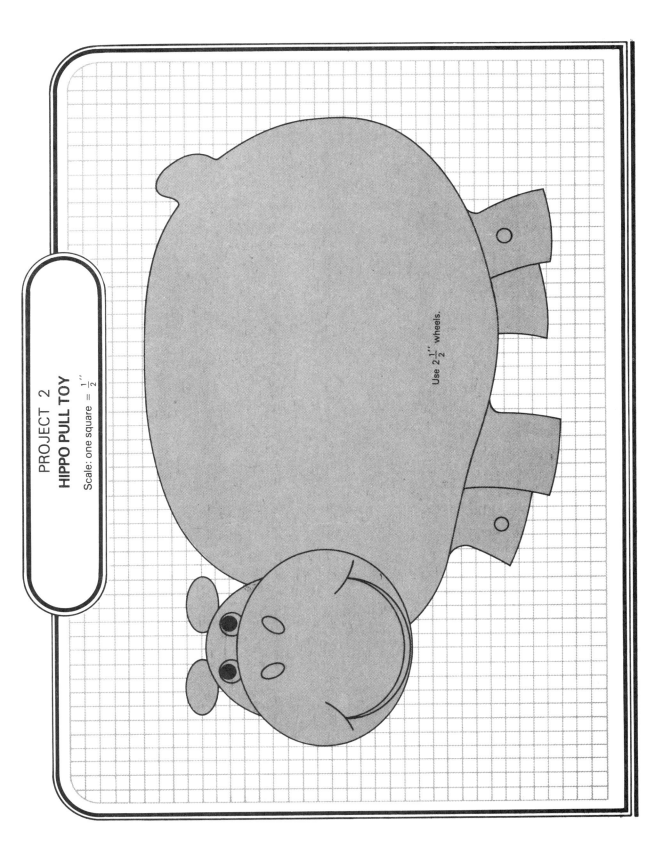

PROJECT 2
HIPPO PULL TOY

Scale: one square = $\frac{1}{2}''$

Use $2\frac{1}{2}''$ wheels.

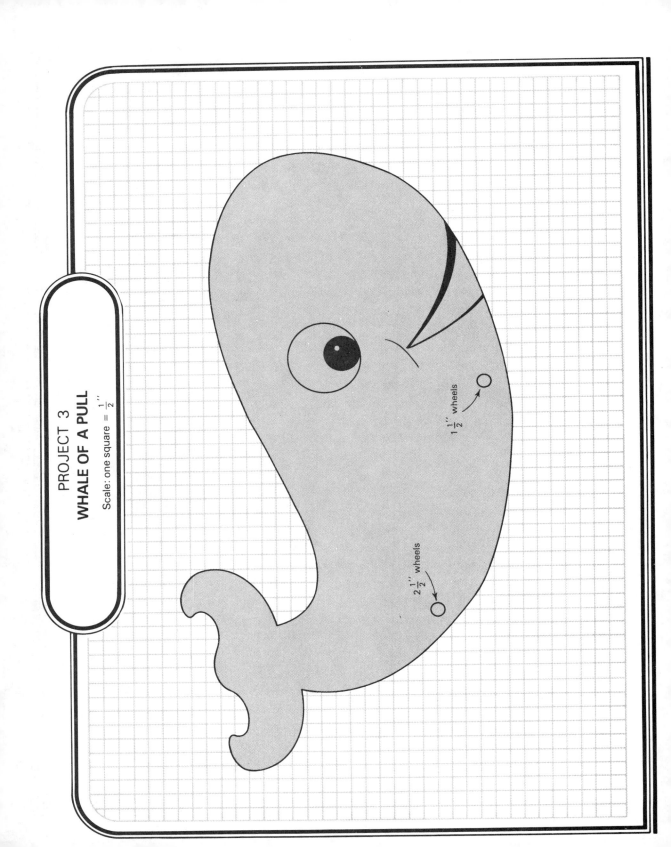

PROJECT 3
WHALE OF A PULL

Scale: one square = $\frac{1}{2}$″

$1\frac{1}{2}$″ wheels

$2\frac{1}{2}$″ wheels

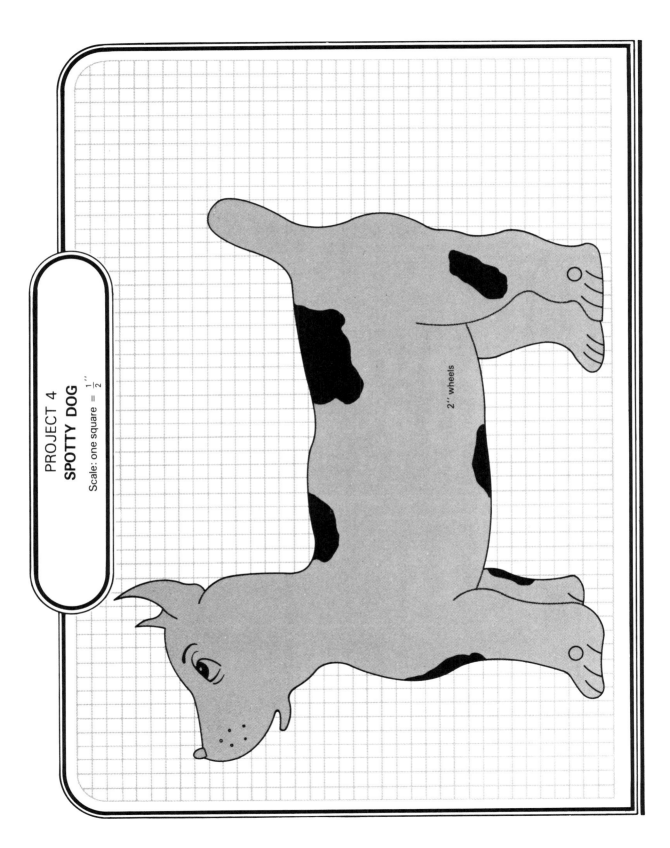

PROJECT 4
SPOTTY DOG

Scale: one square = $\frac{1}{2}''$

2'' wheels

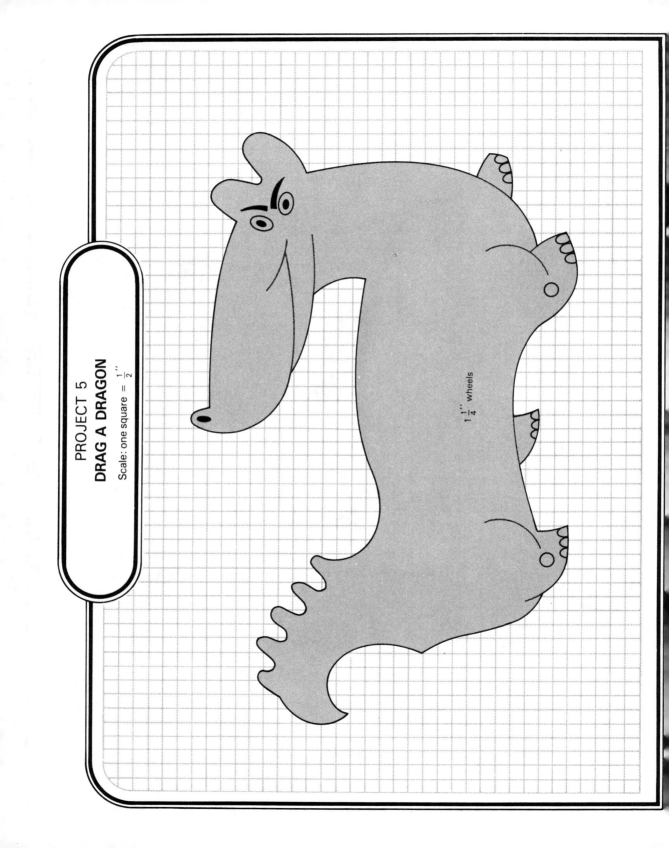

PROJECT 5
DRAG A DRAGON

Scale: one square = $\frac{1}{2}$"

$1\frac{1}{4}$" wheels

Toting Dachshund

This pull toy is a departure, because it is made so that it can be used to carry small objects. Start by making a pad of two pieces of $\frac{1}{2} \times 8 \times 18$-inch plywood. Draw the figure, but before cutting it to shape, locate and drill the holes for the axles.

Next, for the tote assembly, cut two pieces of plywood $\frac{1}{2} \times 2\frac{1}{2} \times 3$ inches and one piece $\frac{1}{2} \times 3 \times 9\frac{1}{2}$ inches and assemble them, as shown in the drawing, with glue and 4d nails.

Attach the sides of the project to the tote assembly by using glue and 4d finishing nails. Set the nail heads and conceal with wood dough. It's a good

The Toting Dachshund has a $\frac{1}{2}$-inch plywood body. The ears and wheels were cut from pine. The axles are hardwood dowels. Finishing was done with a nontoxic sealer.

idea, when doing this part of the job, to have the axles on hand. Put them in place before attaching the sides and they will serve as guides for correct alignment of the two pieces.

To make the ears, draw the pattern on a piece of $\frac{3}{4}$-inch stock. Drill the axle hole, cut the part to shape, and then saw it in half to get two identical parts each about $\frac{3}{8}$ inch thick.

Check the drawing for wheel sizes and for wheel/axle, ear/axle arrangements.

PROJECT 6
TOTING DACHSHUND
Scale: one square = $\frac{1}{2}$ "

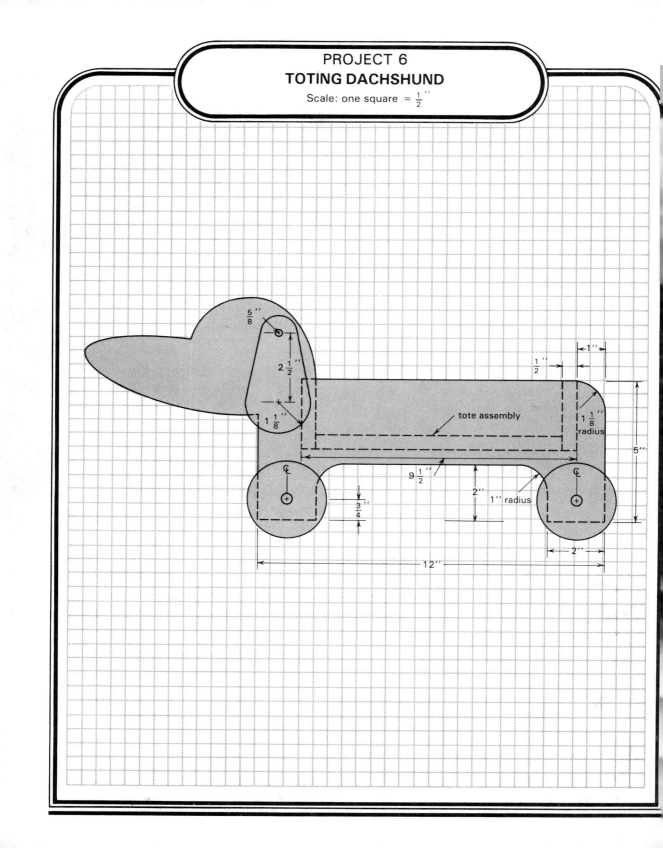

$\frac{5}{8}$ "

$2\frac{1}{2}$ "

$1\frac{1}{8}$ "

tote assembly

$\frac{1}{2}$ "

1 "

$1\frac{1}{8}$ "
radius

5 "

$9\frac{1}{2}$ "

2 "

1 " radius

$\frac{3}{4}$ "

2 "

12 "

PROJECT 6
TOTING DACHSHUND

Scale: one square = $\frac{1}{2}''$

washers

washers

END VIEW

4''

$\frac{1}{2}''$

$\frac{3}{8}''$

$\frac{1}{4}''$

$\frac{1}{2}''$ $2\frac{1}{2}''$

$\frac{3}{4}''$

$\frac{3}{8}''$

$2\frac{3}{4}''$

$\frac{3}{8}''$

$5\frac{3}{4}''$

PULL TOYS WITH ACTION

Hopping Bunny Pull Toy

The bunny seems to hop as it is pulled because the axle holes in the front wheels are offset.

Draw and cut out the animal silhouette in the usual fashion. Make the base from a piece of $\frac{3}{4} \times 3 \times 7\frac{1}{2}$-inch lumber. The centered groove is easy to cut on a table saw, and it can be done with hand tools. But if it's a chore for you, skip it. Just butt-joint the figure to the base. Drill the axle holes

The Hopping Bunny Pull Toy was painted white and detailed with a black, felt-tip pen. The wheels have a natural finish. For a decorative touch on the wheels, apply perfect or erratically cut circles of self-adhesive felt.

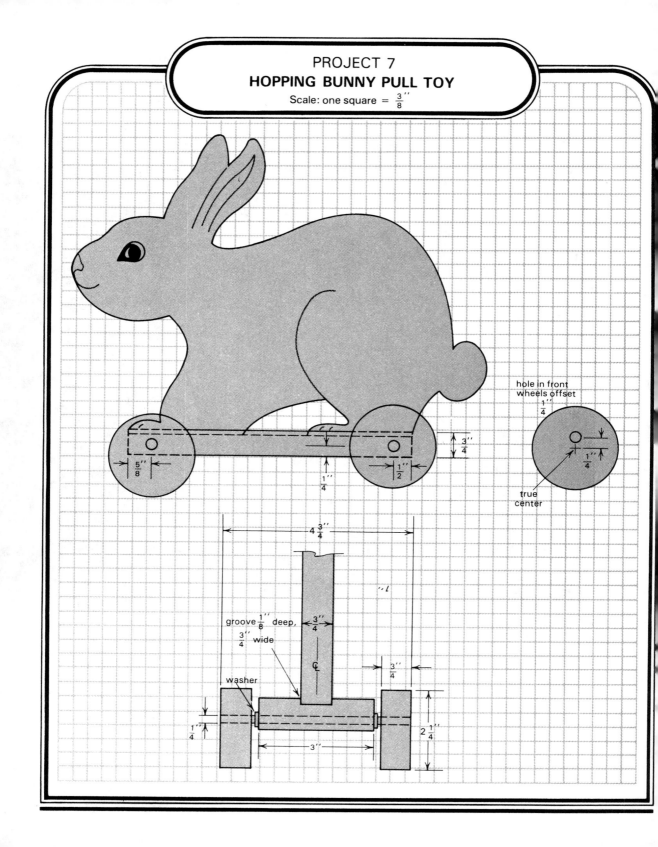

PROJECT 7
HOPPING BUNNY PULL TOY
Scale: one square = $\frac{3}{8}''$

hole in front
wheels offset
$\frac{1}{4}''$

true
center

$\frac{1}{4}''$

$\frac{5}{8}''$

$\frac{1}{4}''$

$\frac{1}{2}''$

$\frac{3}{4}''$

$4\frac{3}{4}''$

$''L$

groove $\frac{1}{8}''$ deep,
$\frac{3}{4}''$ wide

$\frac{3}{4}''$

$\frac{3}{4}''$

washer

$\frac{1}{4}''$

$3''$

$2\frac{1}{4}''$

through the base very carefully. If you are working with hand tools, it may be wise to mark the hole location on each edge of the stock so you can form half-way holes from each edge. Attach the figure to the base with glue and 7d nails.

The axle holes in the rear wheels are center-drilled, but those in the front wheels are offset in the amount shown in the drawing. This will cause an obvious hopping action while still allowing the wheels to turn freely.

The wheel/axle arrangements are detailed in the drawing.

Walking Ducks Pull Toy

This toy employs the cam action that was described on page 92. The bar to which the ducks are attached pivots at one end and has an up-and-down movement, because the free end rests on the eccentric cam rotated by the axle of the front wheels.

Start the project by making the sides and ends of the base and assembling them with glue and small finishing nails. Next, cut the dadoes in the base

The Walking Ducks Pull Toy has a natural finish. All of the round parts were cut from hardwood dowels. The wheels and cam are plywood; other parts are pine. If you have a hole punch you can make small discs of black paper and paste them on as eyes; otherwise, draw the eyes with black ink.

PROJECT 8
WALKING DUCKS PULL TOY

See materials list
for dimensions not
shown on drawing.

about 5°

See Detail D.

See Detail A.

See Detail C.

See Detail B.

metal
washers

DETAIL A (both ends)

$1\frac{1}{8}''$ $\frac{1}{2}''$ $1\frac{1}{8}''$

① ②

DETAIL B

$\frac{1}{4}''$ $\frac{5}{16}''$ ③

$\frac{1}{2}''$

④ ⑧

$\frac{5}{16}''$ hole DETAIL C

$\frac{3}{8}''$ off center

⑨

DETAIL D ⑧ ⑩

project 8
Walking Ducks Pull Toy

MATERIALS LIST

Part No.	Name	Pieces	Size	Material
1	base sides	2	$\frac{3}{4} \times 1\frac{1}{8} \times 10''$	lumber
2	base ends	2	$\frac{3}{4} \times 1\frac{1}{8} \times 3\frac{3}{8}''$	"
3	axle blocks	4	$\frac{3}{4} \times 1\frac{1}{8} \times 1\frac{1}{8}''$	"
4	bar	1	$\frac{3}{4} \times 1 \times 12''$	"
5	necks	2	$\frac{3}{8} \times 5\frac{3}{4}''$	dowel
		2	$\frac{3}{8} \times 5''$	"
6	heads	4	$1\frac{1}{4} \times 1\frac{1}{4}''$	dowel
7	noses	4	$\frac{1}{4} \times 1''$	"
8	axles	2	$\frac{1}{4} \times 5\frac{3}{4}''$	"
9	cam	1	$\frac{3}{4} \times 1\frac{1}{2}''$ dia.	lumber
10	wheels	4	$\frac{3}{4} \times 2\frac{3}{8}''$ dia.	"

Holes through wheels $= \frac{1}{4}''$
Holes through axle blocks $= \frac{5}{16}''$
Hole through cam $= \frac{1}{4}''$
Pivot hole through bar $= \frac{5}{16}''$
Hole in bar and heads for necks $= \frac{3}{8}''$
Holes for noses $= \frac{1}{4}''$

for the axle blocks. Make the axle blocks and use glue to install them in the base.

Cut the bar (part 4 in the drawing) to size. Drill the pivot hole, as shown in Detail C, and the holes for the dowels which serve as necks for the ducks. Make the heads and noses by slicing off sections of dowel, and then drill the head-piece holes. Be sure the pieces are firmly held, regardless of whether you form the holes on a power tool or by hand. Actually, the nose angles are not really critical; they can even differ from head to head. Cut the neck pieces to length and then assemble necks, heads, and noses, and finally, put the assemblies in place on the bar. If the dowels don't fit tightly in the holes you've drilled for them, apply some glue before making the connections.

The next step is to make the axles, wheels, and cam. When you assemble the rear axle and wheels, put the bar in place so the axle will pass through the pivot hole. Detail D in the drawing shows how the cam mounts on the front axle. This too should be placed in the center opening of the base so the front axle can be forced through it. The cam must be a tight fit if it is to turn as the axle turns.

Dog with Waggly Ears

The dog's ears flap happily when the toy is pulled because of the drive wire that runs from the rear wheels to the cam mounted on the ear-axle.

Start the project by drawing the silhouette on one of three pieces of $\frac{3}{4} \times 9\frac{1}{2} \times 13\frac{1}{2}$-inch lumber. Because the total thickness of the parts will be $2\frac{1}{4}$ inches, it will be difficult to saw them as a pad by hand or even with a saber saw or jigsaw. Best bet is to saw a pad of two pieces, and then use one of them as a pattern for the third piece. The center piece of the body is cut as shown by the dotted lines in the drawing. This provides the open area that is needed for the cam and the drive wire.

All of the wooden parts for the Dog with the Waggly Ears are pine lumber. Finishing was done with several coats of sealer. Details were added with a felt-tip pen.

Next, cut all the remaining parts—cam, axles, wheels, and ears. To do the ears, draw the pattern on a piece of $\frac{3}{4}$-inch lumber. After drilling the ear-axle hole and cutting the part to shape, slice it in half so you will have two identical pieces. Before going farther, study Section A-A and Details A and B in the drawing. These show how the cam is mounted and how the rear axle should be shaped.

Put one side of the body and the center pieces together temporarily by using small clamps. You can then mount the cam and rear axle and test to see exactly how long the drive wire must be and whether it has sufficient

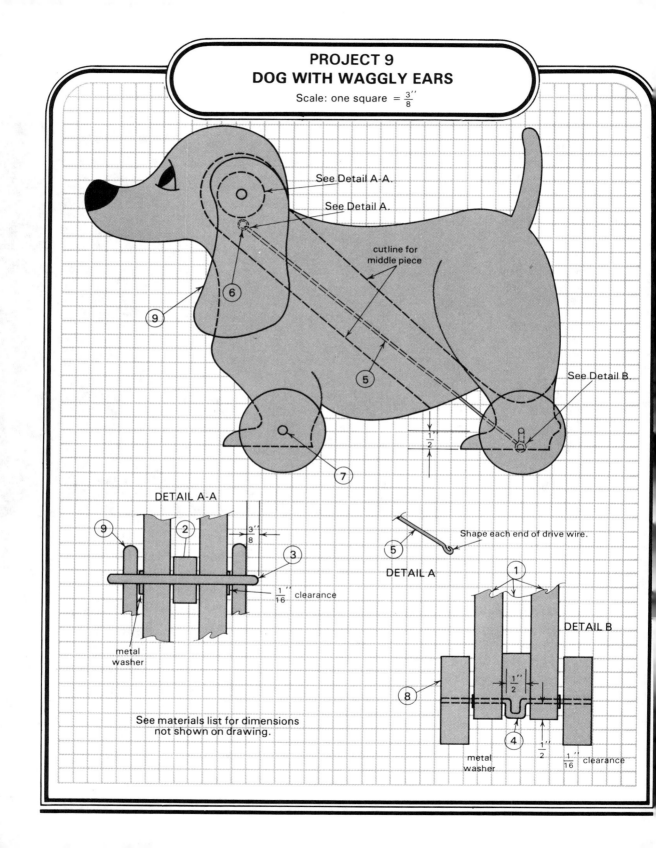

PROJECT 9
DOG WITH WAGGLY EARS

Scale: one square = $\frac{3''}{8}$

See Detail A-A.

See Detail A.

cutline for
middle piece

See Detail B.

$\frac{1''}{2}$

DETAIL A-A

$\frac{3''}{8}$

$\frac{1''}{16}$ clearance

metal
washer

See materials list for dimensions
not shown on drawing.

Shape each end of drive wire.

DETAIL A

DETAIL B

$\frac{1''}{2}$

metal
washer

$\frac{1''}{2}$

$\frac{1''}{16}$ clearance

project 9
Dog with Waggly Ears
MATERIALS LIST

Part No.	Name	Pieces	Size	Material
1	body parts	3	$\frac{3}{4} \times 9\frac{1}{2} \times 13\frac{1}{2}''$	lumber
2	ear cam	1	$\frac{3}{4} \times 1\frac{1}{4}''$ dia.	"
3	ear axle	1	$\frac{1}{4} \times 4''$	dowel
4	rear axle*	1	10 ga. (or $\frac{1}{8}''$) $\times$ 6"	wire
5	drive wire*	1	16 ga. (or $\frac{1}{16}''$) $\times$ 12"	"
6	connector	1	$\frac{1}{4}''$	screweye
7	front axle	1	$\frac{1}{4} \times 4''$	dowel
8	wheels	4	$\frac{3}{4} \times 2\frac{3}{8}''$ dia.	lumber
9	ears	2	$\frac{3}{8} \times 3\frac{1}{2} \times 5\frac{1}{2}''$	"

*Lengths are oversize so parts may be checked on assembly.
Hole through body for front axle $= \frac{5}{16}''$
Hole through front wheels $= \frac{1}{4}''$
Hole through ear cam $= \frac{1}{4}''$
Holes through body for ear axle $= \frac{5}{16}''$
Holes through ears $= \frac{1}{4}''$
Hole in wheels for rear axle $= \frac{3}{32}''$
Hole through body for rear axle $= \frac{5}{32}''$

clearance. When you are satisfied that the action is smooth, you can do the permanent assembly.

The body parts—with the axle-mounted cam, drive wire, and rear axle in place—can be bonded together with glue and clamps, or you can skip the clamping by driving a half dozen or so 6d finishing nails at strategic points around the perimeter from both sides. Set the nail heads and fill the holes with wood dough.

Now add the wheels and ears. Be sure the rear wheels fit very tightly on the axle. We call for a $\frac{3}{32}$-inch hole, which worked fine for the 10 gauge axle-wire used. It might pay to do a test! Drill a hole in some scrap wood and see how the wire you use will fit.

project 10

Elephant with Nodding Head

The elephant will keep nodding as long as he is moved along. The action is caused by the same type of mechanism used on Project 9, except that the drive wire connects to the front axle.

The body consists of four separate pieces—two similar outside pieces, the center piece (or divider), and the head and trunk. You can cut the two similar pieces as one by stacking them. The other two are cut individually

The Elephant with the Nodding Head has a natural finish and black details. The decorative touches are self-adhesive stars that you can buy in a stationery store.

as shown by the dotted lines on the drawing. The lines noted as "marked lines" are details that you can add with a felt-tip pen after the project is assembled. They are not cut-lines.

Because there is access to the mechanism at the front of the toy, there is no need to do a temporary assembly for testing. Mount the head on its axle, and then with the head-axle and the front axle in place, bond the three

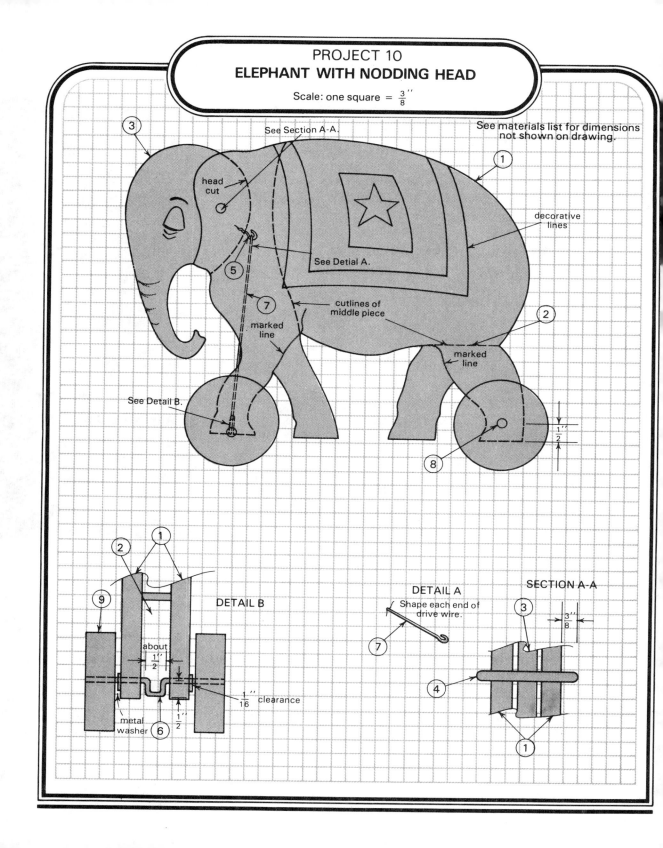

PROJECT 10
ELEPHANT WITH NODDING HEAD
Scale: one square = $\frac{3}{8}$"

See Section A-A.

head cut

See materials list for dimensions not shown on drawing.

decorative lines

See Detial A.

cutlines of middle piece

marked line

marked line

See Detail B.

$\frac{1}{2}$"

DETAIL B

about $\frac{1}{2}$"

$\frac{1}{16}$" clearance

$\frac{1}{2}$"

metal washer

DETAIL A
Shape each end of drive wire.

SECTION A-A

$\frac{3}{8}$"

project 10
Elephant with Waggly Trunk
MATERIALS LIST

Part No.	Name	Pieces	Size	Material
1	body piece (outside)	2	$\frac{1}{2} \times 9 \times 10"$	lumber or plywood
2	body piece (middle)	1	$\frac{3}{4} \times 6\frac{1}{2} \times 7\frac{1}{2}"$	"
3	head	1	$\frac{1}{2} \times 3\frac{3}{4} \times 6"$	"
4	head axle	1	$\frac{1}{4} \times 2\frac{5}{8}"$	dowel
5	connector	1	$\frac{1}{4}"$	screweye
6	front axle*	1	10 ga. (or $\frac{1}{8}"$) $\times 6"$	wire
7	drive wire*	1	16 ga. (or $\frac{1}{16}"$) $\times 7\frac{1}{2}"$	"
8	rear axle	1	$\frac{1}{4} \times 3\frac{5}{8}"$	dowel
9	wheels	4	$\frac{3}{4} \times 2\frac{1}{2}"$ dia.	lumber

*Lengths are oversize so parts may be checked on assembly.
Hole through body for front axle $= \frac{5}{32}"$
Holes in wheels for front axle $= \frac{3}{32}"$
Hole through body for rear axle $= \frac{5}{16}"$
Hole through rear wheels $= \frac{1}{4}"$
Hole through head $= \frac{5}{16}"$
Hole through body for head axle $= \frac{1}{4}"$

body parts together with glue and clamps, or with glue and 3d or 4d finishing nails.

It's a good idea first to form a loop only at one end of the drive wire. Connect it to the screweye in the elephant's head and then manually cause the head to nod so you can judge how long the wire should be. Be sure to place the screweye so that the trunk will not hit the drive wire at the end of the head's down stroke.

Section A-A and Details A and B show the way the head is mounted and the front wheel/axle arrangement.

Rolling Drum Push or Pull Toy

This project intrigues children because the figures (or whatever design you care to use on the drum) rotate as the toy is moved. How you decorate the drum is optional. The figure we used on our project was cut from self-adhesive wallpaper that has designs especially appropriate for a youngster's room. The figure was applied after the drum was painted white.

Start the project by cutting the parts for the base. The axle holes in the sides of the base can be drilled before or after the pieces are assembled. Detail A shows how the base end-pieces are shaped. If you choose to avoid

The figure on the drum was cut from self-adhesive wall paper. There are other ways to decorate. Use a variety of small figures, paint an original design, or draw a spiral. The perimeter of the drum is covered with $\frac{3}{4}$-inch-wide red tape.

The flanges on the rotators might be considered optional, but they make the drum less likely to tip over. The wheels here were cut from hardboard-veneered plywood, but only because there happened to be a scrap piece available. The wheels can be either lumber or plywood.

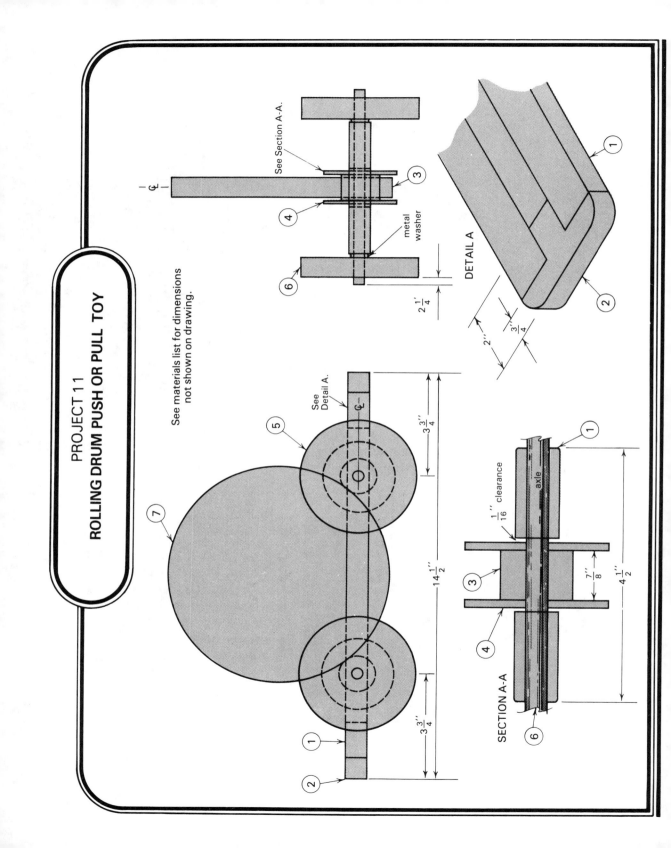

PROJECT 11
ROLLING DRUM PUSH OR PULL TOY

See materials list for dimensions not shown on drawing.

See Section A-A.

metal washer

DETAIL A

$2\frac{1}{4}$

$2''$

$\frac{3}{4}''$

See Detail A.

$3\frac{3}{4}''$

$14\frac{1}{2}''$

$3\frac{3}{4}''$

SECTION A-A

$\frac{1}{16}''$ clearance

axle

$4\frac{1}{2}''$

$\frac{7}{8}''$

project 11
Rolling Drum Push or Pull Toy

MATERIALS LIST

Part No.	Name	Pieces	Size	Material
1	base sides	2	$\frac{3}{4} \times 1\frac{5}{8} \times 13''$	lumber
2	base ends	2	$\frac{3}{4} \times 2 \times 4\frac{1}{2}''$	"
3	rotators	2	$1\frac{1}{4} \times \frac{7}{8}''$	dowel
4	flanges	4	$\frac{1}{8} \times 2\frac{1}{2}''$ dia.	plywood
5	wheels	4	$\frac{3}{4} \times 4''$ dia.	lumber
6	axles*	2	$\frac{3}{8} \times 7''$	dowel
7	drum	1	$\frac{3}{4} \times 7\frac{1}{2}''$ dia.	lumber or plywood

*Length is oversize; trim on assembly.
Holes through base $= \frac{7}{16}''$
Holes through rotators, flanges, and wheels $= \frac{3}{8}''$

the notching that is shown, just use a $\frac{3}{4}$-inch-thick piece and butt-joint it to the ends of the side pieces. In either case, use glue and 6d finishing nails to bond the parts together.

Make the rotators from dowel and the flanges from $\frac{1}{8}$-inch-thick plywood or hardboard. The axle holes can be predrilled in individual pieces, or you can form them after the flanges are glued to the rotators. Remember that the rotator/flange assemblies must be a tight fit on the axles. Put them in place by setting them in the opening in the base and then passing the axle through. The axles will pass easily through the holes in the base, but will have to be tapped with a hammer to pass through the rotator/flange assemblies.

The final construction step is to cut the disc for the drum—which you can do by following one of the methods described beginning on page 74.

Push or Pull Ferris Wheel

This toy takes a bit of time to make, but the results are satisfying. It proved to be one of the favorite action toys among the children who tested these toy projects.

Start the project by doing a careful layout on one of two pieces of $\frac{1}{2} \times$ 7 × 7-inch plywood or lumber. Pad, or stack, the pieces and cut them as one to get two identical parts. Be sure to drill the holes for the seat axles and the main axle before separating the pieces.

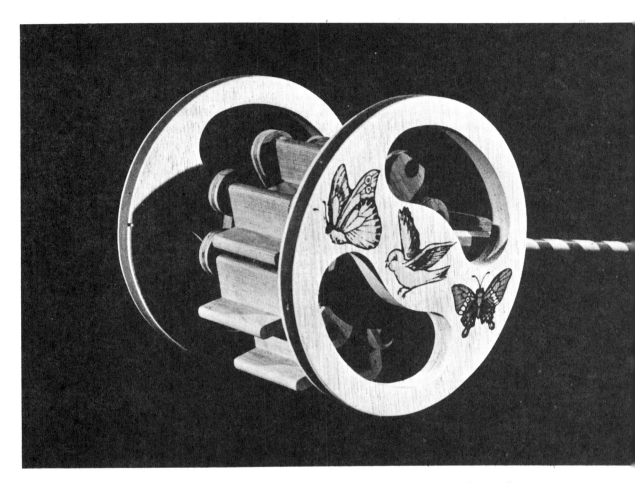

Little David and many other children loved the Ferris Wheel. The handle of the toy was spiral-wound with a colorful tape.

The outside of the main wheels were painted white and then decorated with small figures cut from self-adhesive, children's-room wall paper. The perimeters of the wheels were covered with tape.

The best way to make the seats is to cut a 25- or 26-inch length of $2\times$ 4 (actual size is $1\frac{1}{2} \times 3\frac{1}{2}$ inches) so that it measures $1\frac{1}{2} \times 1\frac{3}{4}$ inches. Then reduce the piece by making a rabbet cut so you will end up with an L-shaped part with leg thicknesses of $\frac{1}{2}$ inch. Then the part can be cut into 3-inch-long sections. If this procedure is a chore for you, make the seats by gluing and nailing together suitably sized pieces of $\frac{1}{2}$-inch stock.

The seat axle holes won't be difficult to form on a drill press. If you work by hand, you will be more accurate if you drill half-way holes from each end. Cut the seat axles to length and then make an assembly of the seats, axles, and ferris wheels. The axles must be a loose fit in the seat holes, but a tight fit in the wheels.

Next, draw the outline of the yoke on a piece of $1\frac{1}{2} \times 5\frac{5}{8} \times 9\frac{1}{4}$-inch lumber and mark the locations of the holes required for the main axle and for the handle. It is best to drill these holes. Drill about $1\frac{3}{4}$ inches deep for the handle hole and about $\frac{3}{4}$ inches deep for the axle holes before cutting the yoke to shape.

Cut the handle to length and insert it into the yoke after coating the end with glue. You can add a couple of 3d finishing nails as reinforcement; just drive them through the yoke so that they penetrate the handle. The handle grip is a ready-made wooden draw pull. It will already have a center for drilling since it is marked for screw attachment. Hold the ball securely with a clamp or in a vise when you form the hole for the handle. Attach the ball with glue.

The main wheels are discs 10 inches in diameter cut from $\frac{3}{4}$-inch-thick plywood or lumber. Make the layout shown in the drawing on one of two pieces that you pad for simultaneous cutting. Be sure to drill the hole for the main axle before separating the pieces.

All you have to do now is the final assembly. Remember that only the main wheels and the ferris wheels must be a tight fit on the main axle. The axle holes through the yoke are large enough so the yoke can pivot freely.

project 12
Push or Pull Ferris Wheel
MATERIALS LIST

Part No.	Name	Pieces	Size	Material
1	ferris wheel	2	$\frac{1}{2} \times 7 \times 7''$	plywood or lumber
2	seats	8	$1\frac{1}{2} \times 1\frac{3}{4} \times 3''$	lumber
3	seat axles	8	$\frac{1}{4} \times 4\frac{1}{2}''$	dowel
4	main axle	1	$\frac{1}{2} \times 8\frac{1}{2}''$	"
5	yoke	1	$1\frac{1}{2} \times 5\frac{5}{8} \times 9\frac{1}{4}''$	lumber
6	handle	1	$\frac{1}{2} \times 21''$	dowel
7	handle grip	1	2'' ball	ready-made draw pull
8	main wheels	2	$\frac{3}{4} \times 10 \times 10''$	plywood or lumber

Holes for seat axles (in ferris wheel) $= \frac{1}{4}''$
Axle hole in seats $= \frac{5}{16}''$
Center hole in ferris wheel $= \frac{1}{2}''$
Hole through yoke (for main axle) $= \frac{9}{16}''$
Hole through main wheels $= \frac{1}{2}''$
Holes for handle in yoke and handle grip $= \frac{1}{2}''$

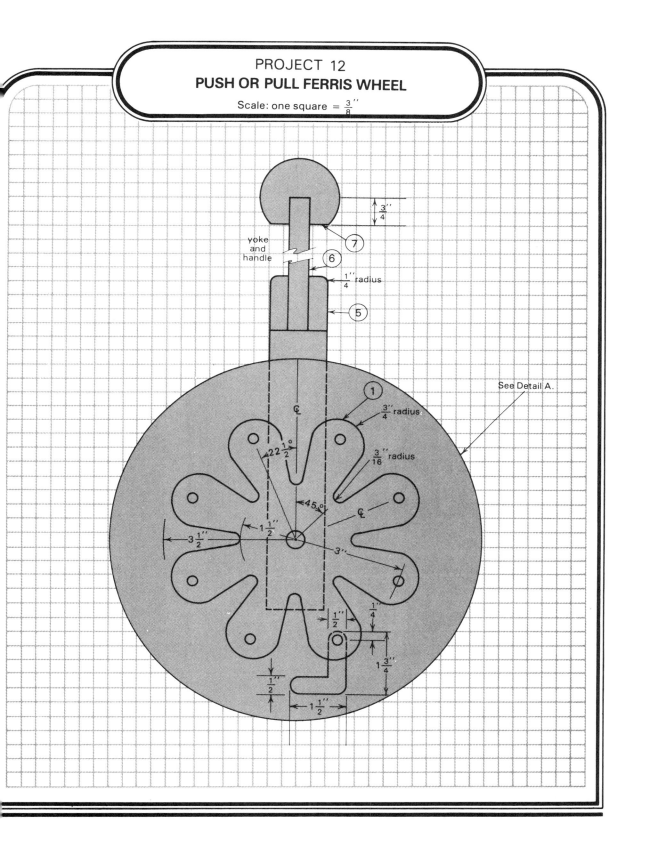

PROJECT 12
PUSH OR PULL FERRIS WHEEL

Scale: one square = $\frac{3}{8}$''

yoke and handle

⑦

⑥

$\frac{1}{4}$'' radius

⑤

$\frac{3}{4}$''

See Detail A.

①

$\frac{3}{4}$'' radius

$\frac{3}{16}$'' radius

$22\frac{1}{2}°$

$45°$

$3\frac{1}{2}''$

$1\frac{1}{2}''$

$3''$

$\frac{1}{2}''$

$\frac{1}{4}$

$1\frac{3}{4}''$

$\frac{1}{2}''$

$1\frac{1}{2}''$

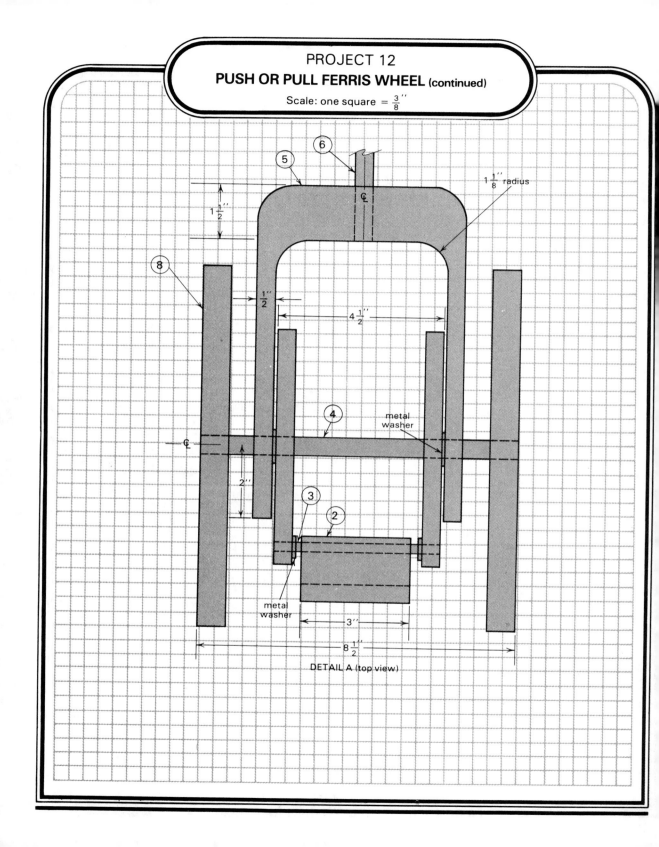

PROJECT 12
PUSH OR PULL FERRIS WHEEL (continued)

Scale: one square = $\frac{3}{8}''$

DETAIL A (top view)

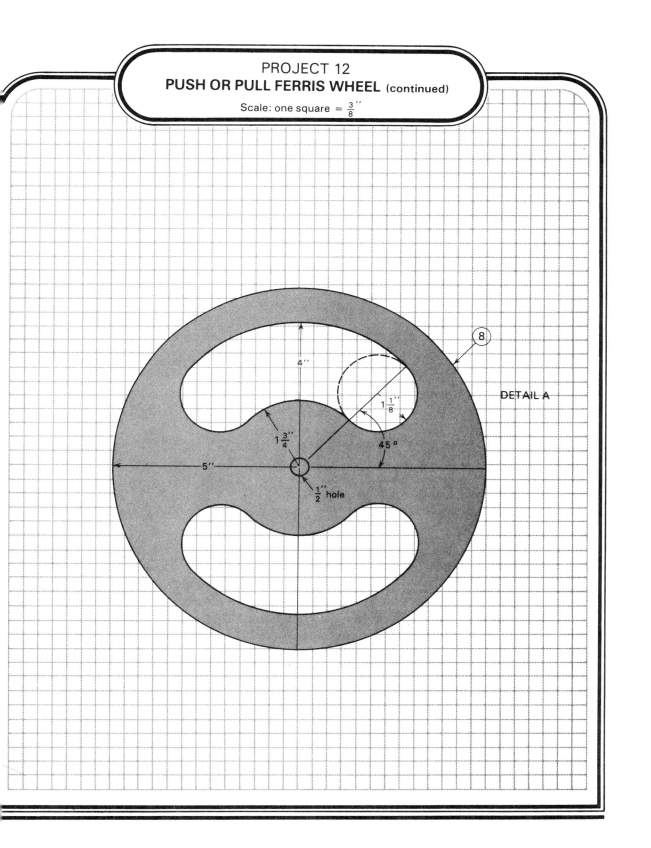

4''

$1\frac{1}{8}$''

8

DETAIL A

$1\frac{3}{4}$''

45°

5''

$\frac{1}{2}$'' hole

Pinwheel Pull Toy

The "pinwheels" of this toy rotate because their axles rest on the perimeter of the wheels that the toy rolls on.

Start the project by forming the body from a piece of $1\frac{1}{2} \times 5\frac{1}{2} \times 11$-inch lumber. It's a good idea to mark the locations for all the axles before you make the angular cuts on the body. Use care when marking hole locations and when drilling. If you're not near perfect, the top wheels may not turn or they may bind.

Cut the discs that are needed for the main wheels, pinwheels, and washers, and after cutting the axles to length, do the final assembly. All the

The body of the toy has a natural finish but its edges are trimmed with colorful tape. The pinwheels are painted, then rimmed with tape, and decorated with black circles, semicircles, and self-adhesive stars. Or you might decide on spirals, figures, or more stars.

wheels must fit tightly on the axles. The axle holes through the body of the toy and the washers are a bit oversize so that axle/wheel assemblies can turn freely.

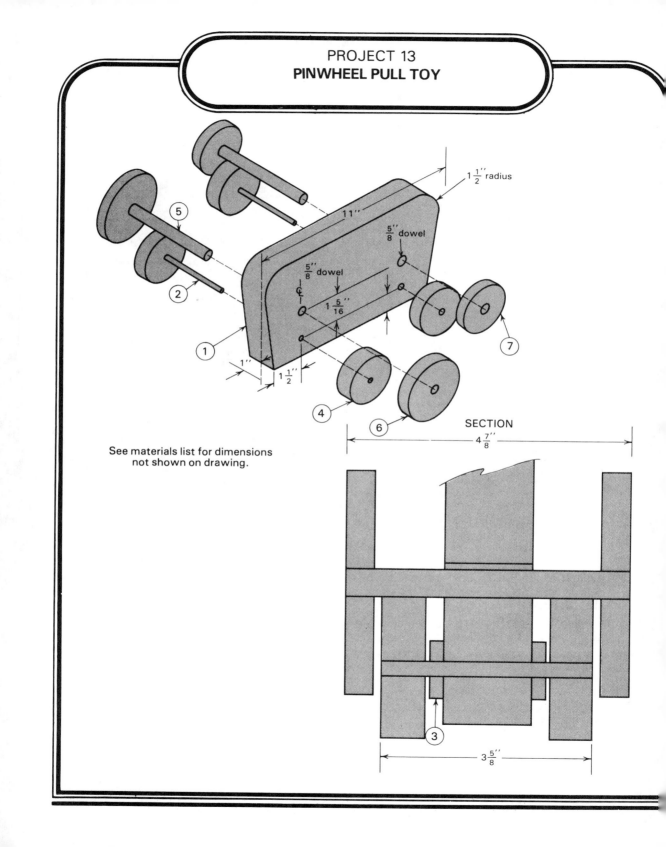

PROJECT 13
PINWHEEL PULL TOY

$1\frac{1}{2}''$ radius

11''

$\frac{5}{8}''$ dowel

$\frac{5}{8}''$ dowel

$1\frac{5}{16}''$

⑤

②

①

1''

$1\frac{1}{2}''$

④

⑥

⑦

SECTION

$4\frac{7}{8}''$

③

$3\frac{5}{8}''$

See materials list for dimensions
not shown on drawing.

project 13
Pinwheel Pull Toy
MATERIALS LIST

Part No.	Name	Pieces	Size	Material
1	body	1	$1\frac{1}{2} \times 5\frac{1}{2} \times 11''$	lumber
2	wheel axles	2	$\frac{1}{4} \times 3\frac{5}{8}''$	dowel
3	washers	4	$\frac{1}{4} \times 1''$ dia.	dowel
4	wheels	4	$\frac{3}{4} \times 2\frac{1}{2}''$ dia.	lumber
5	pinwheel axles	2	$\frac{1}{2} \times 4\frac{7}{8}''$	dowel
6	large pinwheel	2	$\frac{1}{2} \times 4''$ dia.	plywood
7	small pinwheel	2	$\frac{1}{2} \times 2\frac{1}{2}''$ dia.	"

Holes through body for wheels $= \frac{5}{16}''$
Holes through wheels $= \frac{1}{4}''$
Holes through washers $= \frac{5}{16}''$
Holes through body for pinwheel axles $= \frac{5}{8}''$
Holes through pinwheels $= \frac{1}{2}''$

Swiveling Crocodile

Start this project with a 21-inch length of 2×4 (the actual cross-section dimensions will be $1\frac{1}{2} \times 3\frac{1}{2}$ inches). The location of the axle holes, which are pivot points for the body sections, are shown in the lower part of the drawing. Drill these holes and then draw the profile of the crocodile on one surface of the stock. Add the cut-lines that separate the body sections. Saw the figure to profile shape, and then cut the five body pieces.

The inside ends of the head and the tail and both ends of the intermediate pieces are shaped as shown in the top view of the construction drawing.

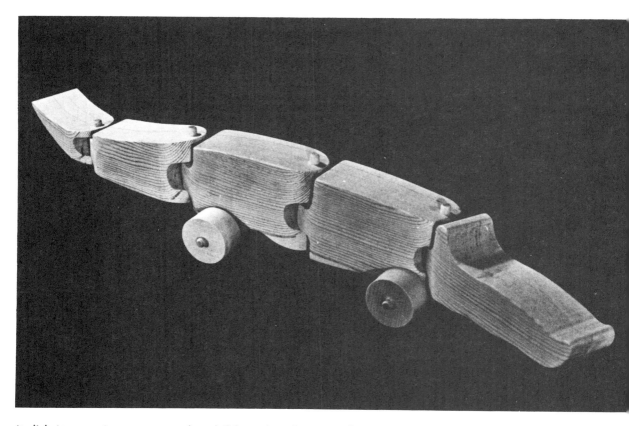

It didn't seem important to the children that the Swiveling Crocodile have a pull cord. They seemed happy just to sit and move the toy about with their hands. All of the parts are pine, except for axles which are hardwood dowels.

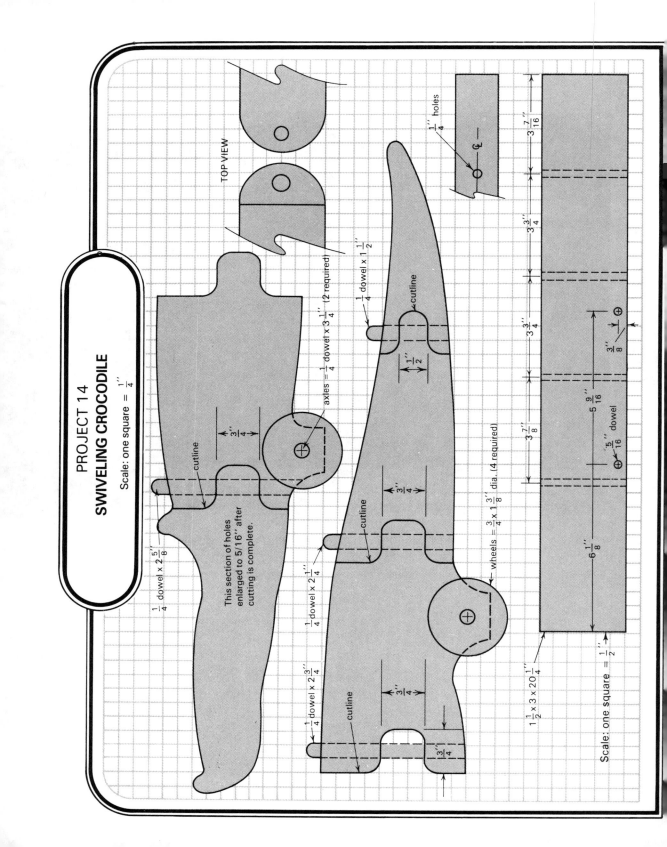

PROJECT 14
SWIVELING CROCODILE

Scale: one square = $\frac{1}{4}$"

TOP VIEW

$\frac{1}{4}$" holes

$\frac{3}{4}$"

cutline

$\frac{1}{4}$ dowel x $2\frac{5}{8}$"

This section of holes enlarged to 5/16" after cutting is complete.

axles = $\frac{1}{4}$ dowel x $3\frac{1}{4}$" (2 required)

$\frac{1}{4}$ dowel x $1\frac{1}{2}$"

cutline

$\frac{1}{2}$"

$\frac{1}{4}$ dowel x $2\frac{1}{4}$"

cutline

$\frac{3}{4}$"

wheels = $\frac{3}{4}$ x 1 $\frac{3}{8}$" dia.. (4 required)

$\frac{1}{4}$ dowel x $2\frac{3}{4}$"

cutline

$\frac{3}{4}$"

$3\frac{7}{16}$"

$3\frac{3}{4}$"

$3\frac{3}{4}$"

$3\frac{7}{8}$"

$\frac{3}{8}$"

$5\frac{9}{16}$"

$\frac{5}{16}$" dowel

$6\frac{1}{8}$"

$1\frac{1}{2}$ x 3 x $20\frac{1}{4}$"

Scale: one square = $\frac{1}{2}$"

Actually, the suggested shape can be modified depending on how much swivel action you feel the joints should have. It's possible to provide enough relief for the body parts to turn at right angles to each other.

The hole in the projecting part of the first four sections is enlarged to $\frac{5}{16}$ inch, so that the pivot dowel is loose in this hole but tight in the holes of the mating section.

After the crocodile's body has been assembled and swivels to your satisfaction, make the wheels and axles and put them in place.

TRUCKS AND CARS

Cab.
Log Carrier.

THE TRUCKING SYSTEM

The Trucking System consists of four projects: a cab and three trailers, each of which is designed for a different function. This was a change from the original design which was just a one-piece sand carrier. The child who tested the vehicle used it in ways that suggested that interchangeable trailers would be more enjoyable.

148

The Cab and Log Carrier. Both projects were painted green except for staves, wheels, and headlights which were left natural. The headlights are faced with discs cut from self-adhesive aluminum tape. The wheel hubs are discs of felt, also self-adhesive, which you can buy ready-made. The wheels are cut from maple.

Start by cutting the bed, or bottom, to size and then drilling the hole for the coupling post. Pad, or stack, two pieces of $\frac{1}{2} \times 5 \times 7$-inch plywood or lumber and then cut them both at once to form the cab sides. Attach these to the base with glue and 4d nails. Cut the back and front, beveling the top edge of the front piece so that it conforms to the angle on the sides. These parts are also attached with glue and 4d nails.

Make and attach the hood and roof. In each case use glue and nails—$\frac{5}{8}$-inch brads for the hood, and 2d or 3d nails for the roof. Attach the axle

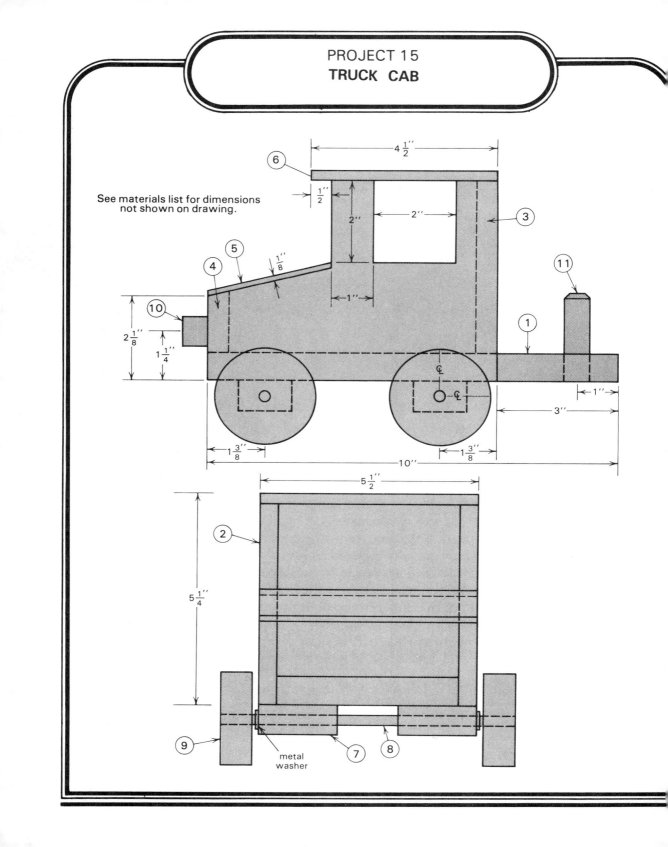

See materials list for dimensions not shown on drawing.

metal washer

project 15
Cab

MATERIALS LIST

Part No.	Name	Pieces	Size	Material
1	bed	1	$\frac{3}{4} \times 4\frac{1}{2} \times 10''$	plywood or lumber
2	sides	2	$\frac{1}{2} \times 5 \times 7''$	"
3	back	1	$\frac{1}{2} \times 4\frac{1}{4} \times 4\frac{1}{2}''$	"
4	front	1	$\frac{1}{2} \times 1\frac{1}{2} \times 4\frac{1}{2}''$	"
5	hood	1	$\frac{1}{8} \times 3\frac{1}{2} \times 5\frac{1}{2}''$	plywood
6	roof	1	$\frac{1}{4} \times 4\frac{1}{2} \times 5\frac{1}{2}''$	"
7	axle blocks	4	$\frac{3}{4} \times 1\frac{1}{4} \times 2''$	lumber
8	axles	2	$\frac{1}{4} \times 7\frac{5}{16}''$	dowel
9	wheels	4	$\frac{3}{4} \times 2\frac{3}{8}''$ dia.	lumber
10	headlights	2	$\frac{3}{4} \times \frac{5}{8}''$	dowel
11	coupling post	1	$\frac{5}{8} \times 2\frac{1}{4}''$	"

Hole through wheels $= \frac{1}{4}''$
Hole through axle blocks $= \frac{5}{16}''$
Hole in bed for coupling post $= \frac{5}{8}''$

blocks with glue and 4d nails. Have the axles on hand so you can insert them in the blocks for correct alignment during assembly.

The headlights are sections of dowel. Drill a small center hole through them so you can easily drive the 3d nail that, with glue, holds them in place. The last step is to make and install the wheels and the coupling pin.

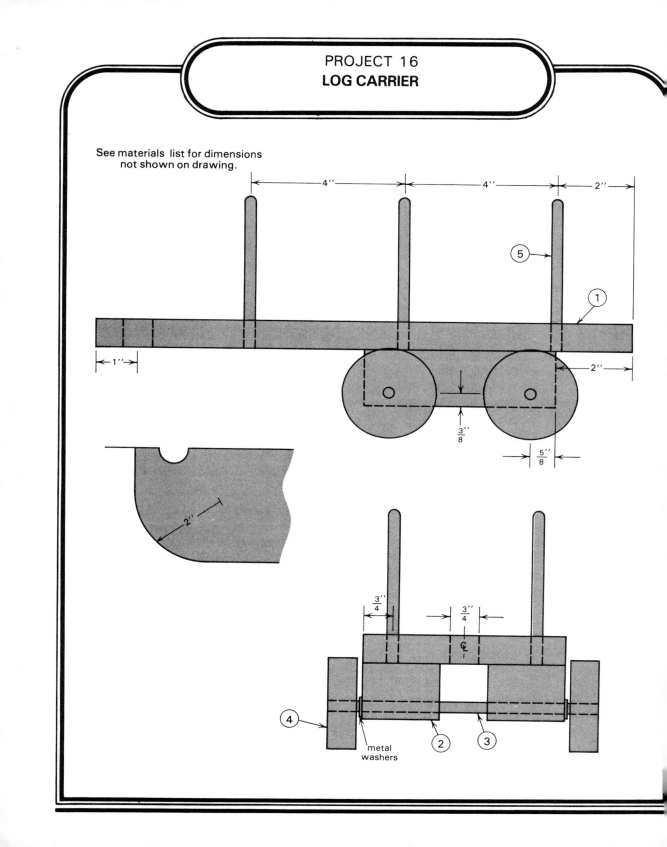

See materials list for dimensions not shown on drawing.

4''   4''   2''

⑤   ①

1''

②   3/8

5/8

2''

3/4   3/4   ℄

④   ② ③

metal washers

project 16
Log Carrier

MATERIALS LIST

Part No.	Name	Pieces	Size	Material
1	bed	1	$\frac{3}{4} \times 6 \times 14$"	plywood or lumber
2	axle blocks	2	$1\frac{1}{2} \times 2 \times 5$"	lumber
3	axles	2	$\frac{1}{4} \times 7\frac{3}{4}$"	dowel
4	wheels	4	$\frac{3}{4} \times 2\frac{3}{8}$" dia.	lumber
5	staves	6	$\frac{1}{4} \times 4$"	dowel

Holes through wheels $= \frac{1}{4}$"
Holes through axle blocks $= \frac{5}{16}$"
Holes in bed for staves $= \frac{1}{4}$"

Cut the bed piece to size, and then drill the $\frac{3}{4}$-inch hole at the front and the $\frac{1}{4}$-inch holes for the staves. Form the axle blocks and put them in place with glue. Nail the blocks down from the top of the bed with 5d or 6d nails. Use the axles as a gauge to be sure the blocks will have correct alignment. Make the staves, taking care to round off the top edges, and put them in place with glue. Then make and attach the wheels.

A parent suggested that the design be changed so that the top ends of the staves would not be exposed. If you feel the point is valid, you can take this extra step. Cut two 9- or 10-inch-long pieces of $\frac{3}{4} \times \frac{3}{4}$-inch stock and in each of them drill three blind holes that are located to suit the spacing of the staves. Sand the pieces to eliminate all sharp edges, and then glue them into place as rails.

Moving Van

Cut the bed to size, shape the front end, and drill the $\frac{3}{4}$-inch hole for the coupling post attachment. You'll note in the drawing that the design calls for rabbet cuts in the sides, front, and roof. These will be easy to form on a table saw, or they can be cut by hand; but if it's too big a chore, you can substitute butt joints. Just be sure that you make necessary dimensional changes.

In either case, the procedure is to attach the sides to the bed; then attach the front, and then the roof. Use glue and nails in all joints. Correct nail lengths will differ depending on whether you have made rabbet or butt joints. A reasonable guide is to choose a nail that is two to three times as long as the thickness of the part being secured.

The Moving Van trailer was finished with several coats of nontoxic sealer. Decorative touches are supplied by strips of $\frac{3}{4}$-inch-wide, white tape.

Make and attach the axle blocks by following the procedure outlined for the Log Carrier. Then cut the back door to size. This should be dressed— that is, reduced in size—just enough so that it will be a loose fit in the opening. Round off the top and bottom edges of the door, and then install its handle.

Use the following procedure to mount the door: Mark the location of the door pivots on the sides of the van and drill a small pilot hole. Hold the

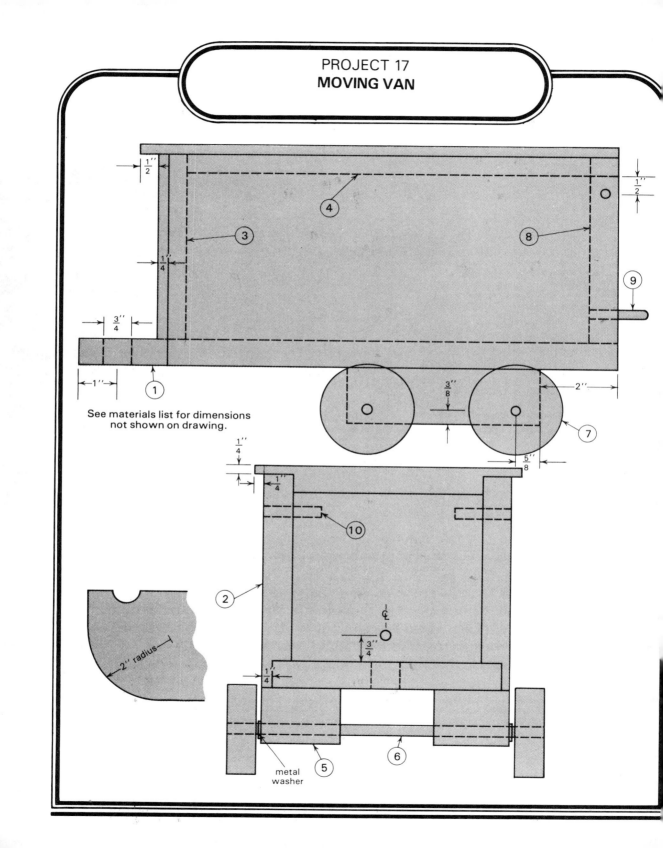

See materials list for dimensions
not shown on drawing.

2'' radius

metal
washer

project 17
Moving Van

MATERIALS LIST

Part No.	Name	Pieces	Size	Material
1	bed	1	$\frac{3}{4} \times 6 \times 14''$	plywood or lumber
2	sides	2	$\frac{3}{4} \times 5\frac{3}{4} \times 11\frac{3}{4}''$	"
3	front	1	$\frac{3}{4} \times 5 \times 6\frac{1}{2}''$	"
4	roof	1	$\frac{3}{4} \times 7 \times 12\frac{1}{2}''$	"
5	axle blocks	2	$1\frac{1}{2} \times 2 \times 5''$	lumber
6	axles	2	$\frac{1}{4} \times 8\frac{1}{4}''$	dowel
7	wheels	4	$\frac{3}{4} \times 2\frac{3}{8}''$ dia.	lumber
8	back door	1	$\frac{3}{4} \times 4\frac{1}{2} \times 5''$	plywood or lumber
9	door handle	1	$\frac{1}{4} \times 1\frac{1}{2}''$	dowel
10	door pivots	2	$\frac{1}{4} \times 1\frac{1}{2}''$	dowel

Hole through wheels $= \frac{1}{4}''$
Hole through axle blocks $= \frac{5}{16}''$
Pivot hole through sides $= \frac{1}{4}''$
Pivot holes in door $= \frac{5}{16}''$
Hole for door handle $= \frac{1}{4}''$

door in position and drill through the pilot holes into the edges of the door. Enlarge the door holes to $\frac{5}{16}$ inch (about 1 inch deep) and the holes in the sides to $\frac{1}{4}$ inch. Put the door in place and tap the door pivots into position. It might be wise to cut the door pivots longer than necessary to begin with. Then you can easily remove them should some adjustment be necessary to prevent the door from binding.

project 18

Sand Carrier

The construction procedure is pretty much the same as that outlined for the preceding projects. Make the bed, then form and install the remaining parts in this order: sides, axle blocks, front, gate, axles, and wheels. The gate is installed in exactly the same manner as the door on the van.

The Sand Carrier trailer has a plywood bed. All body parts are pine. Wheels are maple.

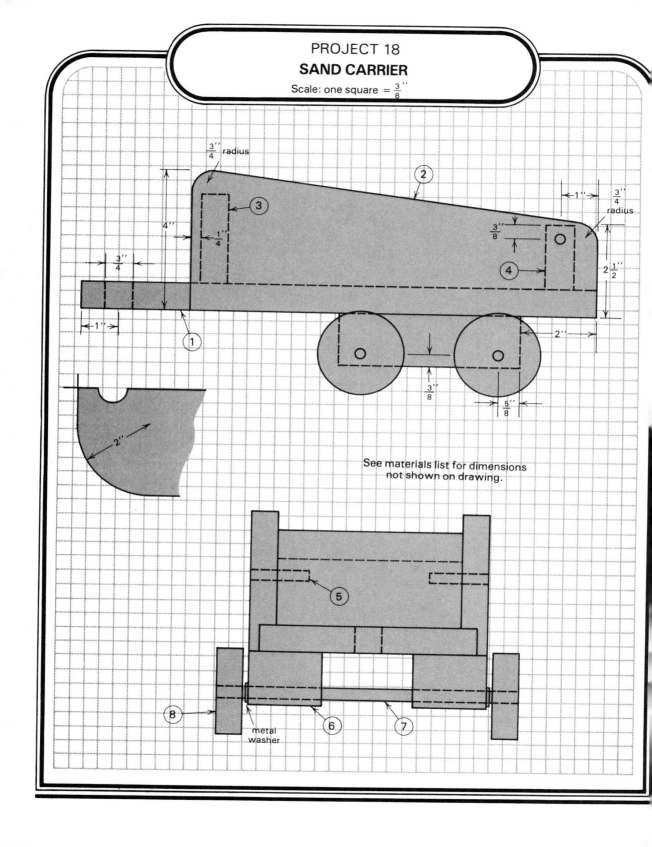

PROJECT 18
SAND CARRIER

Scale: one square = $\frac{3}{8}$"

$\frac{3}{4}$" radius

$\frac{3}{4}$" radius

4"

$\frac{1}{4}$

$\frac{3}{4}$

1"

1"

$\frac{3}{8}$

$2\frac{1}{2}$"

2"

$\frac{3}{8}$

$\frac{5}{8}$"

2"

See materials list for dimensions
not shown on drawing.

metal
washer

project 18
Sand Carrier

MATERIALS LIST

Part No.	Name	Pieces	Size	Material
1	bed	1	$\frac{3}{4} \times 6 \times 14''$	plywood or lumber
2	sides	2	$\frac{3}{4} \times 4 \times 11''$	"
3	front	1	$\frac{3}{4} \times 2\frac{1}{2} \times 5''$	"
4	gate	1	$\frac{3}{4} \times 1\frac{3}{4} \times 5''$	"
5	gate pivots	2	$\frac{1}{4} \times 1\frac{1}{2}''$	dowel
6	axle blocks	2	$1\frac{1}{2} \times 2 \times 5''$	lumber
7	axles	2	$\frac{1}{4} \times 8\frac{1}{4}''$	dowel
8	wheels	4	$\frac{3}{4} \times 2\frac{3}{8}''$ dia.	lumber

Holes through wheels $= \frac{1}{4}''$
Holes through axle blocks $= \frac{5}{16}''$
Pivot hole through sides $= \frac{1}{4}''$
Pivot hole in gate $= \frac{5}{16}''$

Bug.
Sports Car.
Bus.

All three of the projects are made by following a similar procedure. Cut the piece of wood required for the body of the car and then draw the pattern of the car's outline. Mark the location of holes required for windows and axles and drill them as specified on the drawings. Cut the parts to shape of the outline, and then nicely round all edges with sandpaper. The perime-

162

The Bug's body was made from a piece of kiln-dried fir. The wheels are birch. All parts have a natural finish.

ter of the window in the Sports Car is chamfered. This can be done with a file or with sandpaper, and you can also chamfer the windows in the other car projects.

After the bodies are formed, complete the projects by making and adding the wheels and axles. Projects of this nature can be pull toys, but children also seem to enjoy just sitting with them and rolling them about.

You have many options for toy size. There is no reason you can't make any of the cars twice or even three times as large as the drawing suggests.

Materials can be fir, pine, maple, or birch. Often the choice is based on what suitabe-size pieces of scrap wood are available.

PROJECT 19
BUG
Scale: one square = $\frac{1}{4}$″

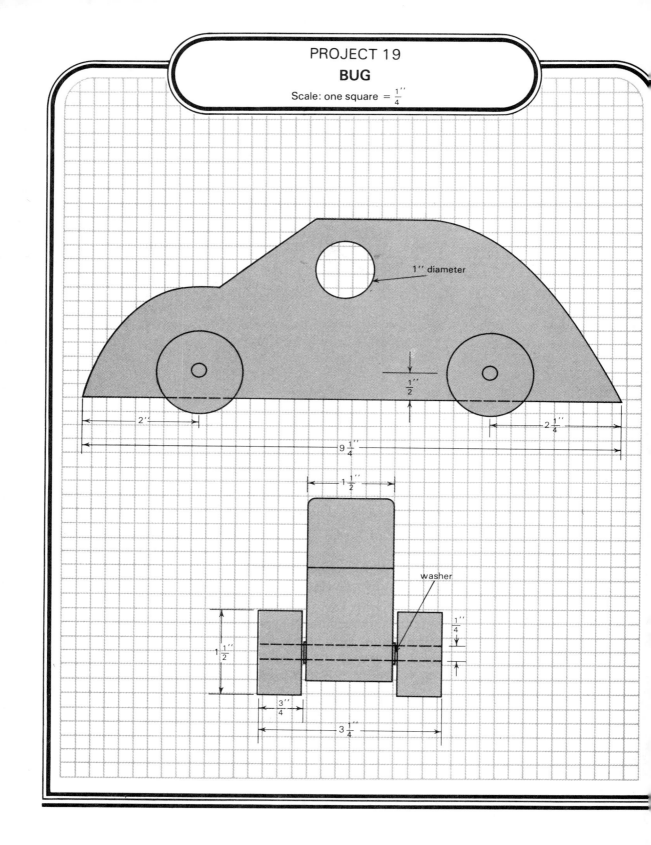

project 19
Bug

MATERIALS LIST

Axles = $\frac{1}{4}$" dowel $\times$ $3\frac{1}{4}$"
Holes through wheels = $\frac{1}{4}$"
Body piece = $1\frac{1}{2} \times 9\frac{1}{4} \times \frac{1}{2}$"
Holes through body = $\frac{5}{16}$"

The Sports Car's body is pine, tinted with diluted, brown mahogany stain. The wheels are teak, but only because I had some small leftovers.

project 20
Sports Car

MATERIALS LIST

Axles = $\frac{1}{4}''$ dowel $\times$ $2\frac{3}{4}''$
Holes through wheels = $\frac{1}{4}''$
Body piece = $1\frac{1}{2} \times 12 \times \frac{3}{8}''$
Holes through body = $\frac{5}{16}''$

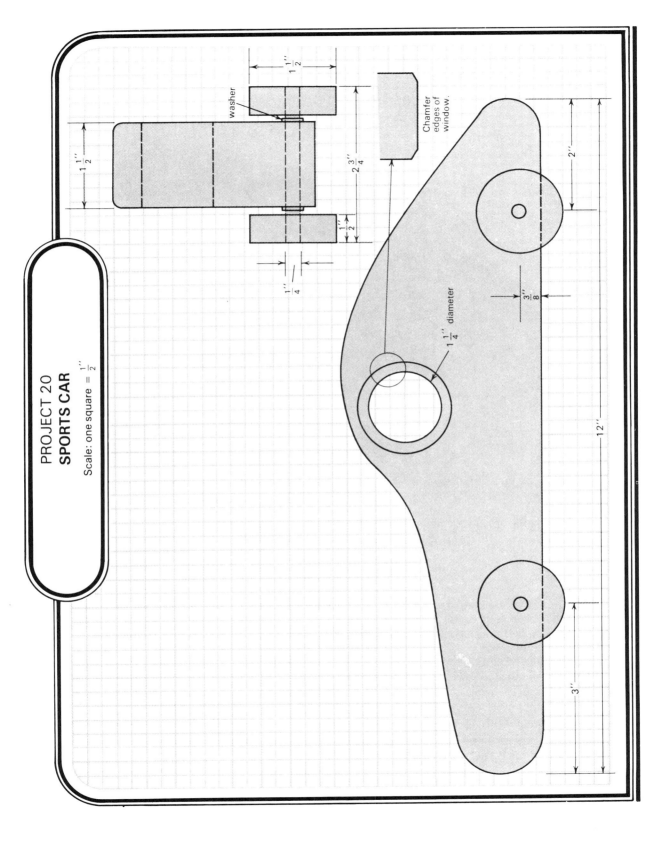

PROJECT 20
SPORTS CAR

Scale: one square = $\frac{1}{2}$''

washer

$1\frac{1}{2}$''

$1\frac{1}{2}$''

$2\frac{3}{4}$''

$\frac{1}{2}$''

$\frac{1}{4}$''

Chamfer edges of window.

$1\frac{1}{4}$'' diameter

$\frac{3}{8}$''

2''

12''

3''

The Bus is kiln-dried fir. The wheels were cut from scrap pieces of cabinet-grade oak plywood.

project 21

Bus

MATERIALS LIST

Axles = $\frac{1}{4}''$ dowel $\times$ $3\frac{1}{4}''$
Holes through wheels = $\frac{1}{4}''$
Body piece = $1\frac{1}{2} \times 4\frac{1}{2} \times 13''$
Holes through body = $\frac{5}{16}''$

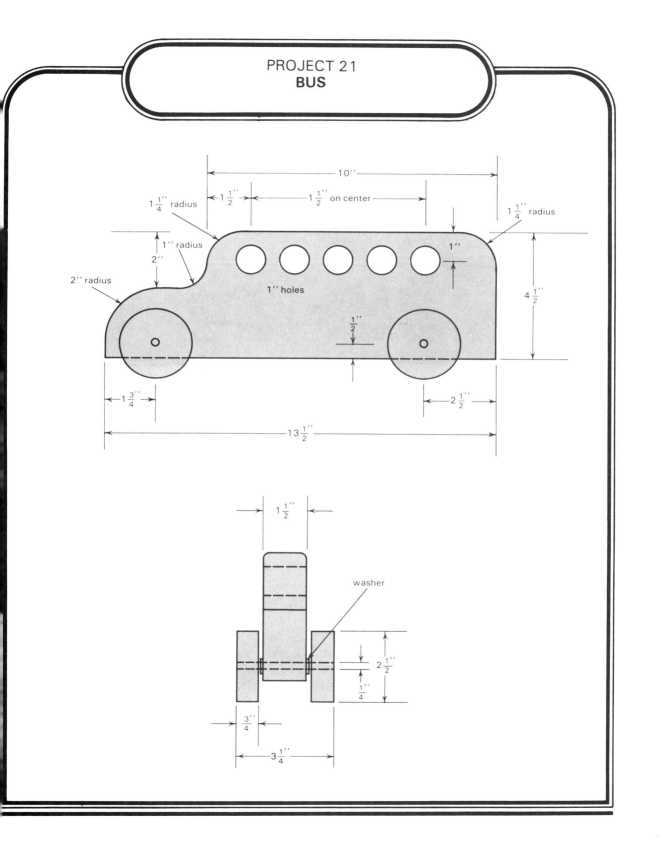

PROJECT 21
BUS

ON-TRACK TRAIN

Locomotive. Passenger Cars. Track.

ON-TRACK TRAIN

The projects consist of a locomotive and a passenger-car design. You can build the locomotive and a single car, but you'll be surprised at how much more enjoyable a child will find the projects when there are more cars—and

170

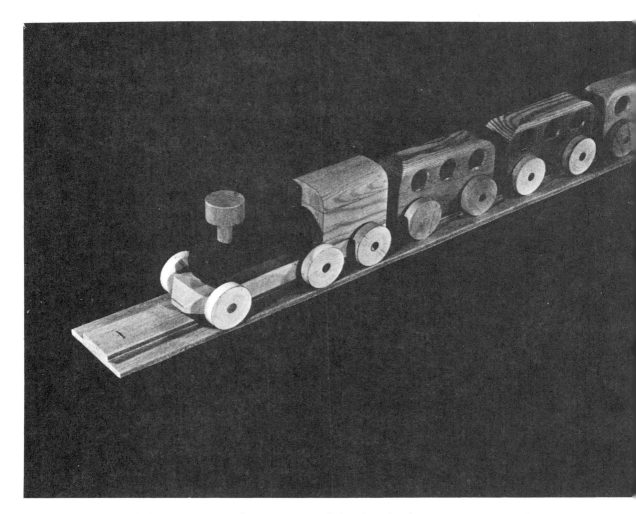

All of the parts of the Long Train have a natural finish. The larger pieces are pine; wheels and axles are hardwood. The boiler is a section of fancy hand rail that was on hand.

the coupling system is easy to use. Pull one car, pull six cars, drop some off to be picked up later—it's all part of the fun of being the engineer.

PROJECT 22
LOCOMOTIVE (for On-Track Train)

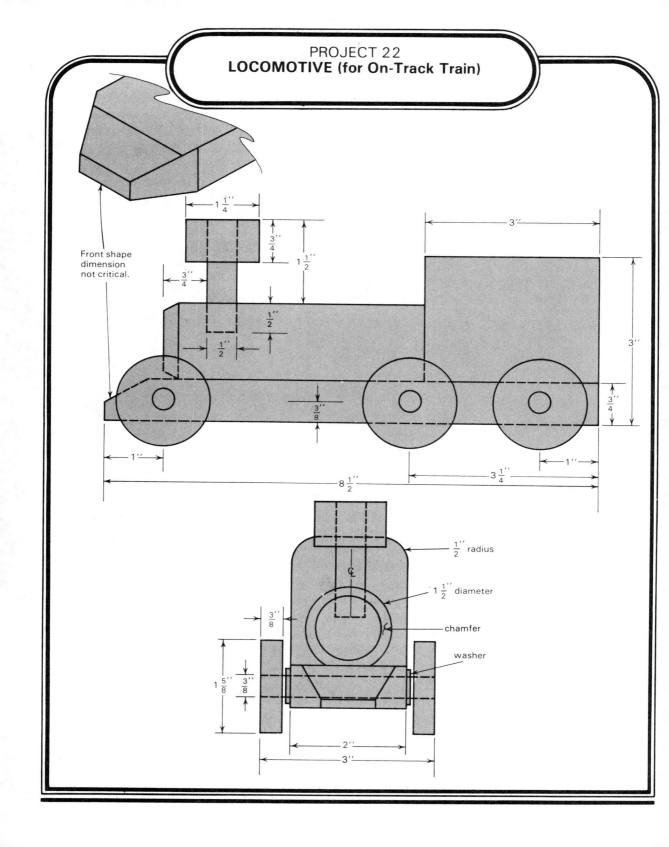

Front shape dimension not critical.

$1\frac{1}{4}''$

$\frac{3}{4}''$

$1\frac{1}{2}''$

$\frac{3}{4}''$

$\frac{1}{2}''$

$\frac{1}{2}''$

3''

3''

$\frac{3}{4}''$

$\frac{3}{8}''$

1''

$8\frac{1}{2}''$

$3\frac{1}{4}''$

1''

$\frac{1}{2}''$ radius

$1\frac{1}{2}''$ diameter

chamfer

washer

$\frac{3}{8}''$

$1\frac{5}{8}''$

$\frac{3}{8}''$

2''

3''

project 22

Locomotive

MATERIALS LIST

Axles = $\frac{3}{8}''$ dowel $\times$ 3"
Holes through wheels = $\frac{3}{8}''$
Holes through body = $\frac{7}{16}''$

The bed, or bottom, is a piece of $2 \times 8\frac{1}{2} \times \frac{3}{4}$-inch stock. Shape the front end as shown in the drawing, paying more attention to the form than to any particular dimension. Locate and drill the holes for the axles. The cab measures $2 \times 2\frac{1}{4} \times 3$ inches. You can cut it from a piece of 4×4 or make it by gluing together pieces cut from a 2×4. Round off its top edges, and then attach the cab to the bed with glue and 6d nails driven up through the bottom of the bed.

The boiler can be made from a round or lathe-turned cylinder, or it can be a length of hand rail. The flat on a round can be formed with a plane or by using a rasp and then sanding. Drill the hole for the stack and then attach the boiler to the bed as you did for the cab. Make the stack assembly, glue it into place, and then add axles and wheels.

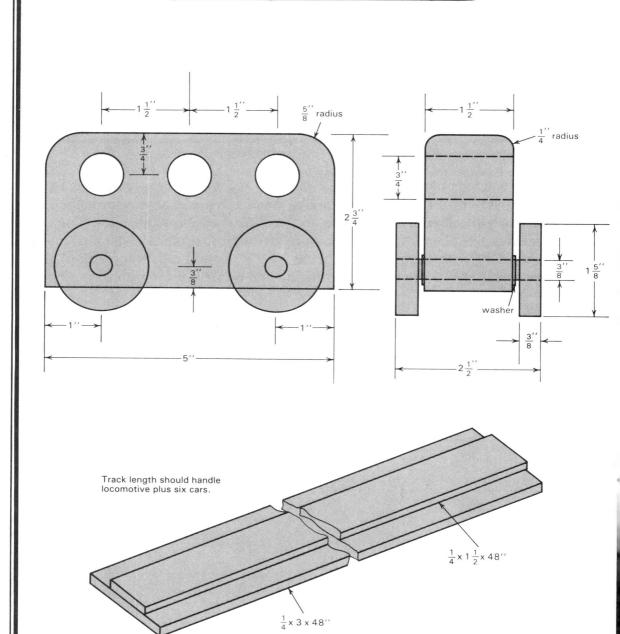

$\frac{5}{8}''$ radius

$1\frac{1}{2}''$ $1\frac{1}{2}''$

$\frac{3}{4}''$

$2\frac{3}{4}''$

$\frac{3}{8}''$

$1''$ $1''$

$5''$

$1\frac{1}{2}''$

$\frac{1}{4}''$ radius

$\frac{3}{4}''$

$\frac{3}{8}''$ $1\frac{5}{8}''$

washer

$\frac{3}{8}''$

$2\frac{1}{2}''$

Track length should handle
locomotive plus six cars.

$\frac{1}{4}$ x $1\frac{1}{2}$ x 48''

$\frac{1}{4}$ x 3 x 48''

project 23

Passenger Cars

MATERIALS LIST

Axles = $\frac{3}{8}''$ dowel $\times$ $2\frac{1}{2}''$
Holes through wheels = $\frac{3}{8}''$
Holes through body = $\frac{7}{16}''$

Cut a number of pieces (I made six) of $1\frac{1}{2}$-inch-thick stock to measure $2\frac{3}{4} \times 5$ inches. Form the two top ends on each piece to about a $\frac{5}{8}$-inch radius, and then work with sandpaper to round off all edges. Mark the locations of the window and axle holes on one piece. Drill pilot holes and then use the piece as a template to mark hole locations on the other parts. This is easy to do if you hold the template piece against another and pass the drill bit through the pilot holes.

Open the holes to full size, and then make and install the axles and wheels.

The track goes where the Long Train goes. The coupling system consists of a small screweye in one car, a small screw hook in the following one. If the screw hooks you buy have sharp points, blunt them with a file.

project 24

Track

MATERIALS LIST

Track length suitable for locomotive plus six cars
Material $= \frac{1}{4}''$ plywood

The track is made by assembling two pieces of $\frac{1}{4}$-inch plywood. The plywood can be glued and then held with clamps, or you can substitute $\frac{1}{2}$-inch staples for the clamps.

My original thought was that the child could use the track to display the On-Track Train when he wasn't playing with it, but it became as important in his play activities as the train itself. In fact, we're being harassed to build more track, even curved ones!

THE TRAIN

Locomotive.
Tender.

This locomotive has a lot more detail than the one designed for the On-Track Train; so it will take more time and care to make.

Start by forming the bed from a piece of $\frac{3}{4} \times 3\frac{3}{4} \times$ 16-inch stock. Shape the back and front ends, and then drill the hole for the coupling pin. Make and attach the cab's sides with glue and 3d or 4d nails. The front and the roof are rabbeted as the drawing shows, but an alternative method is to use butt joints. If you use butt joints, make any necessary dimensional changes. The front can still be $\frac{1}{2}$-inch stock, but it will be better to use $\frac{1}{4}$-inch material for the roof.

The drive rod adds interest to the Train project. All parts have a natural finish.

The boiler's diameter is $2\frac{1}{2}$ inches, and it's not likely that you'll find that size in a ready-made round. It can be made on a lathe, or it can even be made by hand if you start with square stock, cutting off corners with a saw and finishing with a plane and sandpaper. That will take some time, but it can be done. Another solution is to check the ready-made spindles available in do-it-yourself centers to see if you can cull a suitable piece. When the part is on hand, drill it for the stacks, and then attach it to the bed with glue and 5d or 6d nails driven up through the bottom of the bed.

Make and attach the axle blocks with glue and 5d nails. If you have the axles on hand, they can be used to help you make sure the blocks are correctly aligned. Shape a piece of wood to the cow-catcher form shown on the drawing. The angles don't have to be perfect. Attach the part with glue and 5d nails driven up through the bottom of the bed.

Now you can make and install the stacks and headlight. The headlight will be easier to attach if you first drill a small center hole for a 5d or 6d nail.

PROJECT 25
LOCOMOTIVE (for the Train)

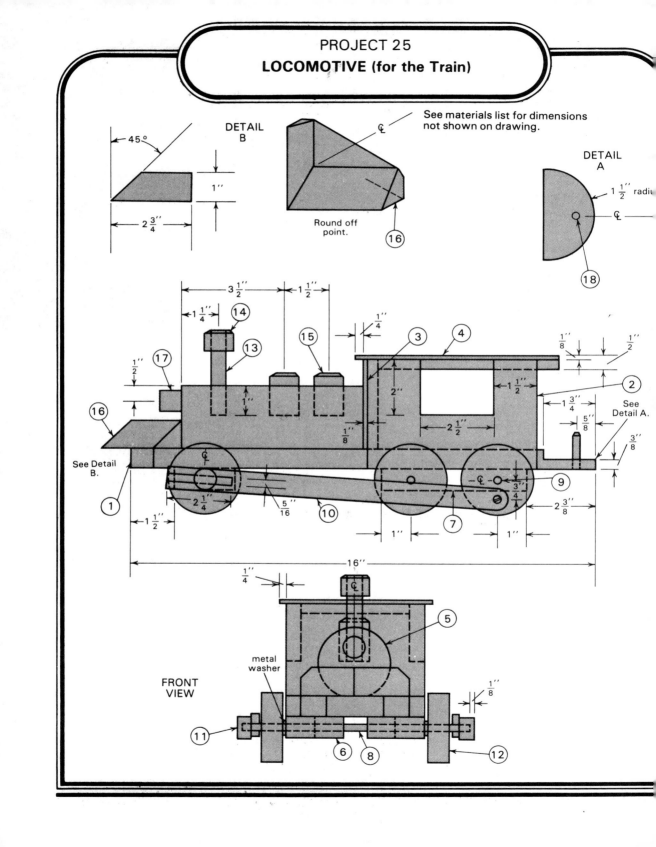

DETAIL B

45°

1''

2 3/4''

See materials list for dimensions not shown on drawing.

Round off point.

16

DETAIL A

1 1/2'' radius

18

3 1/2''

1 1/2''

1 1/4''

14

15

1/4''

3

4

1/8''

1/2''

13

17

1/2''

1''

2''

1 1/2''

1 3/4''

2

See Detail A.

16

1/8''

2 1/2''

5/8''

See Detail B.

1

C

2 1/4''

5/16''

10

1''

7

C

3/4''

9

2 3/8''

3/8''

1''

1 1/2''

16''

FRONT VIEW

1/4''

C

5

metal washer

1/8''

11

6   8

12

project 25
Locomotive

MATERIALS LIST

Part No.	Name	Pieces	Size	Material
1	bed	1	$\frac{3}{4} \times 3\frac{3}{4} \times 16''$	lumber
2	cab sides	2	$\frac{1}{2} \times 4 \times 6''$	lumber or plywood
3	cab front	1	$\frac{1}{2} \times 3\frac{1}{4} \times 4\frac{3}{4}''$	"
4	cab roof	1	$\frac{1}{2} \times 5\frac{1}{4} \times 7''$	"
5	boiler	1	$2\frac{1}{2}''$ dia. $\times 6\frac{1}{4}''$	lumber (turned)
6	front axle blocks	2	$\frac{3}{4} \times 2 \times 2''$	lumber
7	rear axle blocks	2	$\frac{3}{4} \times 1 \times 5''$	"
8	front axle	1	$\frac{1}{4} \times 8''$	dowel
9	rear axles	2	$\frac{1}{4} \times 6\frac{5}{8}''$	"
10	drive rod	2	$\frac{1}{4} \times \frac{3}{4} \times 12''$	lumber
11	front axle caps	2	$\frac{3}{4} \times \frac{1}{2}''$	dowel
12	wheels	6	$\frac{3}{4} \times 2\frac{3}{8}''$ dia.	lumber
13	tall stack	1	$\frac{1}{2} \times 3''$	dowel
14	tall stack cap	1	$1''$ dia. $\times \frac{3}{4}''$	dowel
15	short stacks	2	$1''$ dia. $\times 1\frac{1}{2}''$	"
16	cow catcher	1	$1 \times 2\frac{3}{4} \times 3\frac{3}{4}''$	lumber
17	headlight	1	$\frac{3}{4} \times \frac{3}{4}''$	dowel
18	coupling pin	1	$\frac{1}{4} \times 1\frac{1}{4}''$	dowel

Holes through wheels = $\frac{1}{4}''$
Holes through axle blocks = $\frac{5}{16}''$
Hole for coupling pin = $\frac{1}{4}''$

Make the drive rods, cutting the slots at the front end just wide enough to avoid binding the axle. Make and install the axles and wheels, and then add the drive rod. Use a $\frac{5}{8}$- or $\frac{3}{4}$-inch round- or pan-head screw to attach the rod to the rear wheel. The screw, of course, merely acts as a pivot; don't

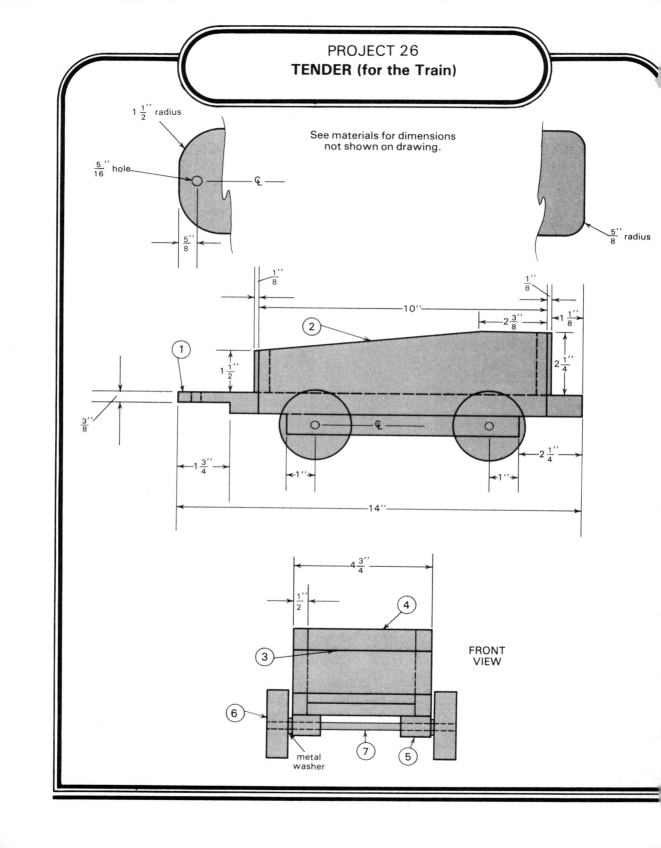

$1\frac{1}{2}''$ radius

See materials for dimensions
not shown on drawing.

$\frac{5}{16}''$ hole

$\frac{5}{8}''$

$\frac{5}{8}''$ radius

$\frac{1}{8}''$

10''

$2\frac{3}{8}''$

$\frac{1}{8}''$

$1\frac{1}{8}''$

$1\frac{1}{2}''$

$2\frac{1}{4}''$

$\frac{3}{8}''$

$1\frac{3}{4}''$

1''

1''

$2\frac{1}{4}''$

14''

$4\frac{3}{4}''$

$\frac{1}{2}''$

FRONT
VIEW

metal
washer

tighten it. Drill the hole through the drive rod just large enough for the rod to move freely.

Make the front axle caps by drilling a $\frac{1}{4}$-inch-deep center hole in pieces of $\frac{3}{4}$-inch dowel that are $\frac{1}{2}$ inch thick. Glue them in place at the ends of the front axle. There must be enough clearance between the wheel and the cap so that the drive rod will move without binding.

project 26
Tender

MATERIALS LIST

Part No.	Name	Pieces	Size	Material
1	bed	1	$\frac{3}{4} \times 3\frac{3}{4} \times 14''$	lumber
2	sides	2	$\frac{1}{2} \times 3 \times 10''$	lumber or plywood
3	front	1	$\frac{1}{2} \times 1\frac{1}{2} \times 4\frac{3}{4}''$	"
4	back	1	$\frac{1}{2} \times 2\frac{1}{4} \times 4\frac{3}{4}''$	"
5	axle blocks	2	$\frac{3}{4} \times 1 \times 8''$	lumber
6	wheels	4	$\frac{3}{4} \times 2\frac{3}{8}''$ dia.	"
7	axles	2	$\frac{1}{4} \times 6\frac{5}{8}''$	dowel

Holes through axle blocks $= \frac{5}{16}''$
Holes through wheels $= \frac{1}{4}''$

Cut the bed to size, then shape the front and rear ends and drill the hole that will couple the tender to the locomotive. Make and attach the sides to the bed with glue and 4d nails. Add the front and the back. These pieces are rabbeted, but butt joints may be substituted if you change dimensions to suit. Form and drill the axle blocks, and attach them with glue and 4d nails driven from the bottom of the blocks. Then make and install the axles and wheels.

GAMES

Tick-Tack-Toe Board and Men

TICK-TACK-TOE PLUS GAME

Tick-Tack-Toe will be more fun to play on a special board with posts and "game-men" of various shapes than on paper with pencils. The version here includes two extra, small projects that extend the fun and can also be used as teaching aids.

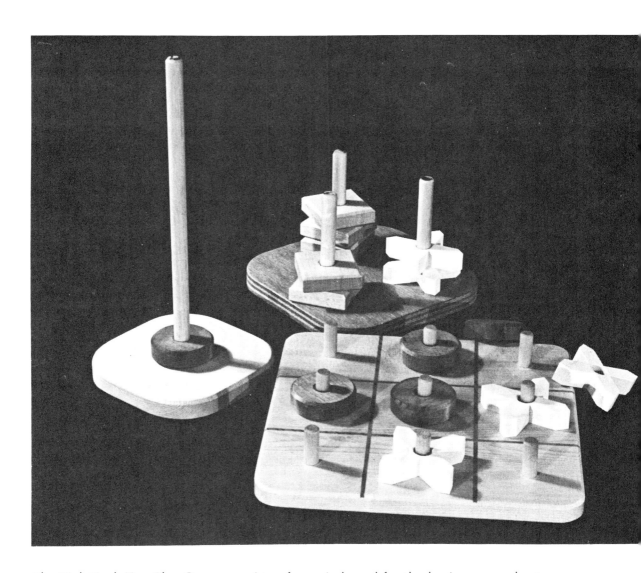

The Tick-Tack-Toe Plus Game consists of a main board for the basic game, plus two extra projects that add to the fun and can be used as teaching aids.

PROJECT 27
TICK-TACK TOE BOARD AND MEN

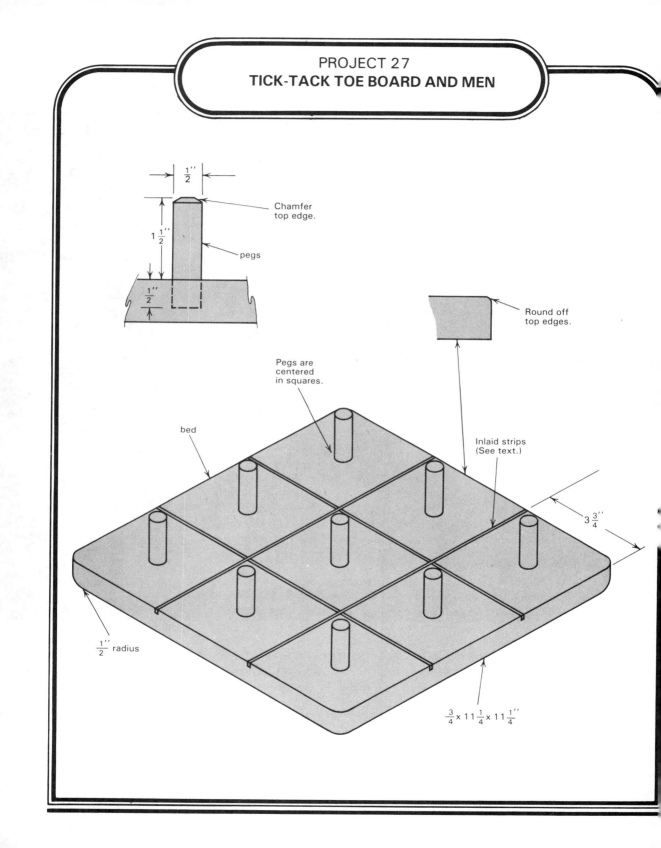

$\frac{1}{2}''$

Chamfer
top edge.

$1\frac{1}{2}''$

pegs

$\frac{1}{2}''$

Round off
top edges.

Pegs are
centered
in squares.

bed

Inlaid strips
(See text.)

$3\frac{3}{4}''$

$\frac{1}{2}''$ radius

$\frac{3}{4} \times 11\frac{1}{4} \times 11\frac{1}{4}''$

Start by cutting a piece of $\frac{3}{4}$-inch-thick lumber to measure $11\frac{1}{4}$ inches square. I inlaid strips to divide the board into squares by following this procedure on a table saw: Set the blade's height to project about $\frac{1}{8}$ inch. Lock the rip fence so that the distance to the blade (which will actually be the center of the kerf the blade cuts) is $3\frac{3}{4}$ inches. Cut one groove, then turn the stock so the opposite edge is against the fence, and cut a second groove. Cut strips from a contrasting material to fit the grooves and glue them into place. The thickness of the strips will depend on how wide a kerf the blade cuts. A good procedure is to cut strips as wide as the kerf from a piece of, say, $\frac{1}{2}$-inch-thick stock. The strips can then be sliced lengthwise with a sharp knife. After the strips are in place, the excess projecting above the board can be sanded flush.

With the first two strips in place, repeat the kerf cutting procedure for the two grooves that cross the first ones. Then install the second set of strips. When you work this way, the joints where the strips cross will be perfect. The grooves can also be formed with a hand saw, or you can avoid them entirely by marking the board into squares with paint or ink or by applying narrow strips of self-adhesive tape.

Draw diagonals connecting opposite corners of each square to locate centers and then drill the "blind" holes for the posts. Cut the posts to length, round off or chamfer their top ends, and glue them into place.

(Continued)

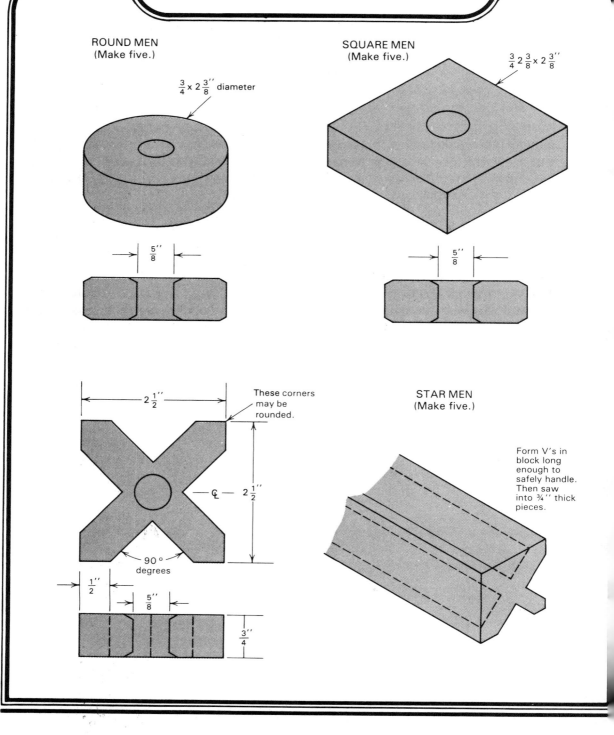

ROUND MEN
(Make five.)

$\frac{3}{4} \times 2\frac{3}{8}''$ diameter

$\frac{5}{8}''$

SQUARE MEN
(Make five.)

$\frac{3}{4}$ $2\frac{3}{8} \times 2\frac{3}{8}''$

$\frac{5}{8}''$

$2\frac{1}{2}''$

These corners
may be
rounded.

₵ — $2\frac{1}{2}''$

$90°$
degrees

$\frac{1}{2}''$

$\frac{5}{8}''$

$\frac{3}{4}''$

STAR MEN
(Make five.)

Form V's in
block long
enough to
safely handle.
Then saw
into ¾'' thick
pieces.

THE MEN

The round and the square men are fairly easy to make; the star men take a little more doing. If you work on a table saw, you can start with a $2\frac{1}{2}$-inch square block of wood that is long enough to handle safely. Cut V-grooves down the center of each side, and then slice off as many $\frac{3}{4}$-inch-thick pieces as you want. If you work with hand saws, it will be better to make individual $\frac{3}{4}$-inch-thick by $2\frac{1}{2}$-inch-square pieces and then cut the V-shapes in each. With a band saw you can cut V-grooves in stock that is long enough to be sliced into the number of parts that are needed.

Single Post

The single post can be used to stack the men haphazardly or in some alternating pattern of shapes or colors. It can also be used to teach counting and the meaning of numbers. Put on three stars and one round and one square, and how many pieces do you have?

The project is simply a base with a centered $\frac{1}{2}$-inch dowel $12\frac{1}{2}$ inches long.

All parts of the Single Post, except for the hardwood-dowel post, were made from pine lumber. The star men are white, the round ones are stained, and the square ones have a natural finish. You can use brighter colors if you wish.

$\frac{1}{2}''$

chamfer

12''

$\frac{1}{2}''$

2'' radius

Round off
top edges.

$\frac{3}{4} \times 6 \times 6''$

Triple Post

This too is used with the Tick-Tack-Toe men for play or used like the Single Post as a teaching aid. Cut the base to shape, and draw a 5-inch-diameter circle around its center. The center of the holes for the posts are 120 degrees apart on the circumference of the circle.

The base of the Triple Post project is plywood, but lumber will do just as well. It can be used as a teaching aid for distinguishing shapes and colors.

TRIPLE POST (a take-off from the Tick-Tack-Toe Game)

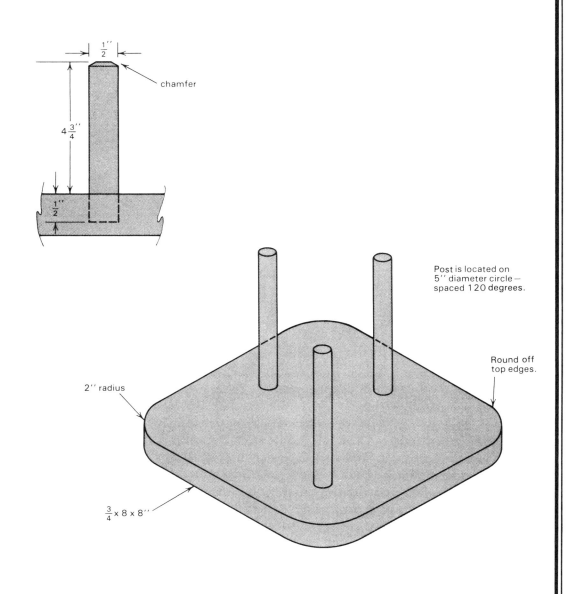

$\frac{1}{2}''$

chamfer

$4\frac{3}{4}''$

$\frac{1}{2}''$

Post is located on
5'' diameter circle —
spaced 120 degrees.

Round off
top edges.

2'' radius

$\frac{3}{4} \times 8 \times 8''$

Spiral Game

The object of spiral games is to tilt the wooden base to make the ball travel the length of the spiral without falling off. Skilled players may want to compete for time.

Start the project with a piece of cabinet-grade plywood $\frac{3}{4}$ inch thick and 12 inches square. Draw diagonals from opposite corners of the square to locate the center, and drill a $\frac{1}{4}$-inch hole at that point. Make the spiral marker shown in the drawing. The string, which can be stapled to both the pencil holder and the dowel, should be just long enough so the starting radius of the spiral will be $5\frac{5}{8}$ inches. The pencil should have a slip fit so that the holder can rest flat on the work. The string wraps around the dowel

The waste that results when you cut the spiral groove in the square piece can be used to make a second project. The spiral-cut pieces are mounted on plywood or hardboard bases. A natural finish is suitable.

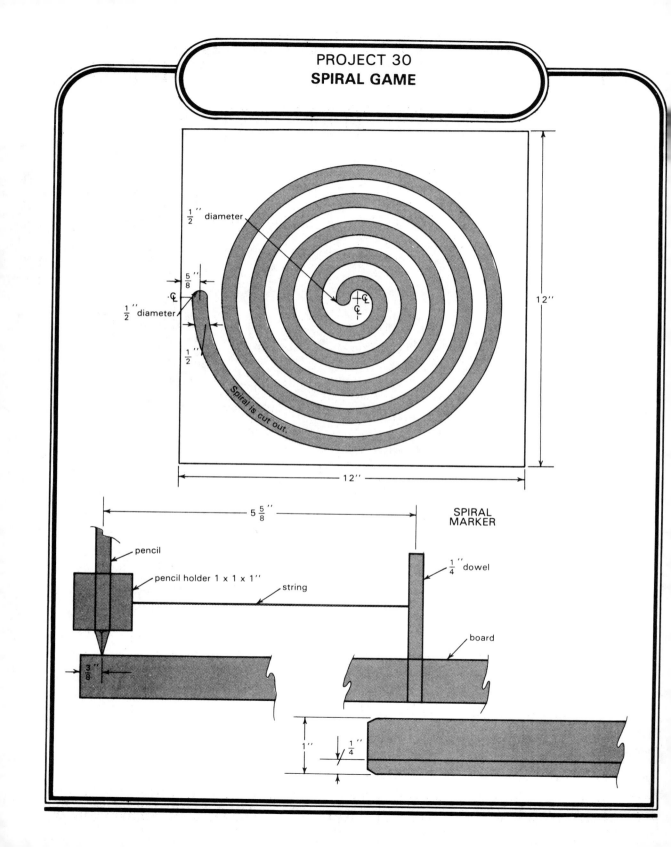

PROJECT 30
SPIRAL GAME

$\frac{1}{2}''$ diameter

$\frac{5}{8}''$

$\frac{1}{2}''$ diameter

$\frac{1}{2}''$

Spiral is cut out.

12''

12''

$5\frac{5}{8}''$

SPIRAL MARKER

pencil

pencil holder 1 x 1 x 1''

string

$\frac{1}{4}''$ dowel

board

$\frac{3}{8}''$

1''

$\frac{1}{4}''$

as you rotate the holder to produce the spiral pattern. Be sure to keep the string taut.

The next step is to drill the $\frac{1}{2}$-inch hole at the start of the spiral. Be sure to locate its center at the center of the spiral track. Use the hole to insert the blade of whatever tool you will saw with—saber saw, jigsaw, deep-throat coping saw. Don't try to be overly precise in making the cut. Some slight irregularities will add to the difficulty of playing the game.

When the cut is complete, place the work on a bench and use a compass to draw a second parallel spiral. Set the compass to a $\frac{1}{2}$-inch width and keep the point of the compass in the saw-cut as a guide.

The second cut you make results in a $\frac{1}{2}$-inch-wide spiral groove in the square piece and a spiral-shaped waste piece that can be used for a second game. The spiral-cut piece is mounted on a base of $\frac{1}{4}$-inch plywood or hardboard. Coat mating surfaces with glue and then hold them together with a weight of some sort until the glue is dry. The result is another spiral-pattern groove and a second game to play with.

Zig-Zag Traveler

The toy in the photos has one traveling piece, but there are others you can add to increase interest. For example, substitute small jig-sawed figures for the block or use a steel rod instead of a dowel. The extra weight of the steel will often cause a hesitation at the top of a slope which reverses the pinwheel's direction of rotation.

Start by making a pad of two pieces of $6 \times 14 \times \frac{1}{2}$-inch-thick plywood or lumber. Drill the hole in the upper right-hand corner for the $\frac{3}{8}$-inch-diameter dowel tie, and then make the layout for the zig-zag route. Do the cutting very carefully—you want a smooth path for the traveler. The waste

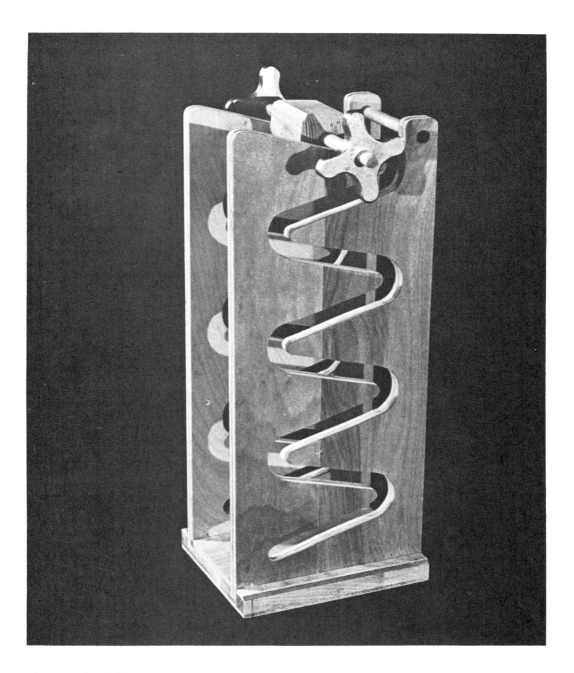

The traveler follows a zig-zag path down the sides of the toy.

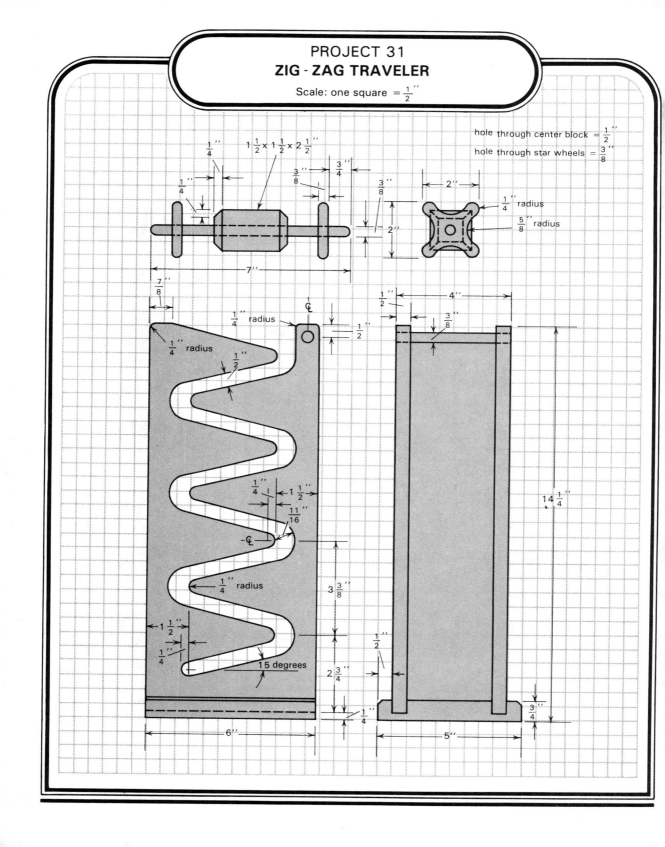

PROJECT 31
ZIG - ZAG TRAVELER

Scale: one square = $\frac{1}{2}''$

You can make travelers in addition to the one shown here. A little experimenting should prompt you toward a few original designs.

material has an interesting pattern, and should be stored for possible use on a future project.

The base—plywood or lumber—measures $\frac{3}{4} \times 5 \times 6$ inches and is grooved to receive the sides. Install the sides by using glue and driving a few 3d nails up through the bottom of the base. Add the dowel tie, meanwhile checking to be sure the sides of the project are parallel.

Construction details of the traveler are shown in the drawing. It will be easy to make duplicate star wheels if you draw the pattern on a piece of $\frac{3}{4}$-inch stock and then slice the piece into two parts after the star's outline has been formed. The star wheels fit tightly on the axle; the center block does not.

Marble Ride

Teddy, age 12, was so impressed with this project and the Marble Roller Coaster **(Project 33)** which comes next, he found it difficult to wait until he could take complete possession. Interestingly, he tried to keep marbles constantly moving while his brother David, age 4, was content to let a marble run the entire course before starting another.

The best way to begin construction is to make the *returns* that are shown in Detail A in the drawing. Cut 6 pieces of stock (a few back-ups won't hurt) so they measure $1\frac{1}{2}$ inch square and 3 inches long. Bore a $\frac{3}{4}$-inch-diameter center hole in each piece $2\frac{1}{2}$ inches deep. Next, as shown in Step 3, bore a $\frac{3}{4}$-inch hole through one wall of the return. Then, working with a file or something similar, form the semicircular opening at the bottom of

All main parts of the Marble Ride have a natural finish. Decorative touches were added with self-adhesive tapes and stars. The banner was painted and then titled with the self-adhesive letters sold in stationery stores. The flag poles, which are removable, have a spiral-winding of colorful tape.

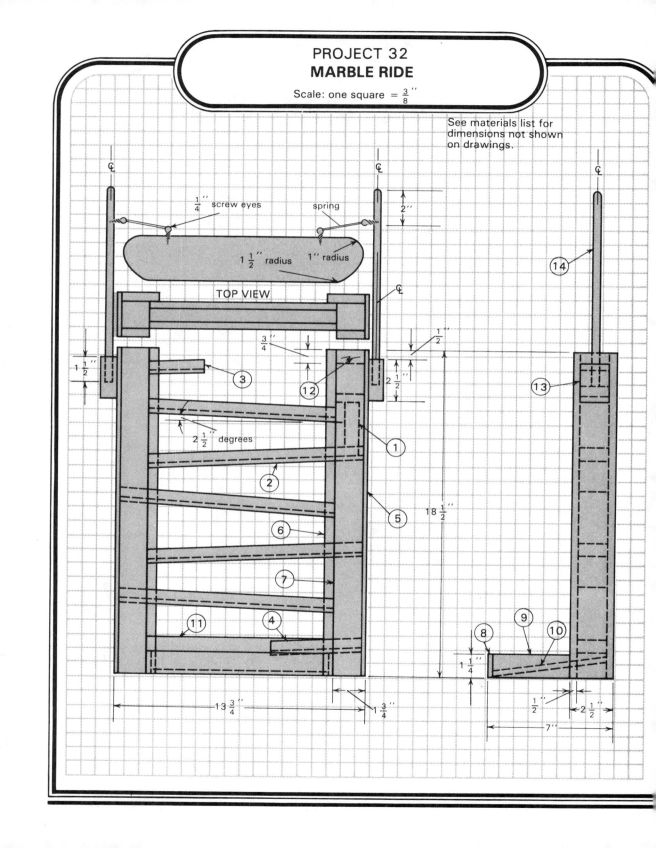

PROJECT 32
MARBLE RIDE

Scale: one square = $\frac{3}{8}$''

See materials list for dimensions not shown on drawings.

$\frac{1}{4}$'' screw eyes

spring

2''

$1\frac{1}{2}$'' radius   1'' radius

TOP VIEW

$\frac{3}{4}$''

$\frac{1}{2}$''

$1\frac{1}{2}$''

14

3

12

$2\frac{1}{2}$''

13

$2\frac{1}{2}$'' degrees

1

2

5

18$\frac{1}{2}$''

6

7

11   4

9

8   10

$1\frac{1}{4}$''

13$\frac{3}{4}$'' $1\frac{3}{4}$''

$\frac{1}{2}$'' $2\frac{1}{2}$''

7''

PROJECT 32
MARBLE RIDE (continued)

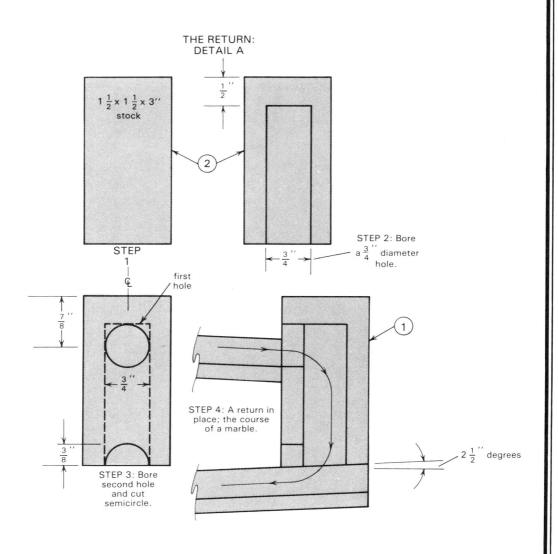

THE RETURN:
DETAIL A

$\frac{1}{2}''$

$1\frac{1}{2} \times 1\frac{1}{2} \times 3''$ stock

STEP 1

STEP 2: Bore a $\frac{3}{4}''$ diameter hole.

$\frac{3}{4}''$

first hole

$\frac{7}{8}''$

$\frac{3}{4}''$

$\frac{3}{8}''$

STEP 3: Bore second hole and cut semicircle.

STEP 4: A return in place; the course of a marble.

$2\frac{1}{2}''$ degrees

THE RUN:
DETAIL B

$11\frac{3}{4}''$

$1\frac{1}{2}''$

$\frac{3}{8}''$

$\frac{1}{2}''$

② 2

CROSS
SECTION

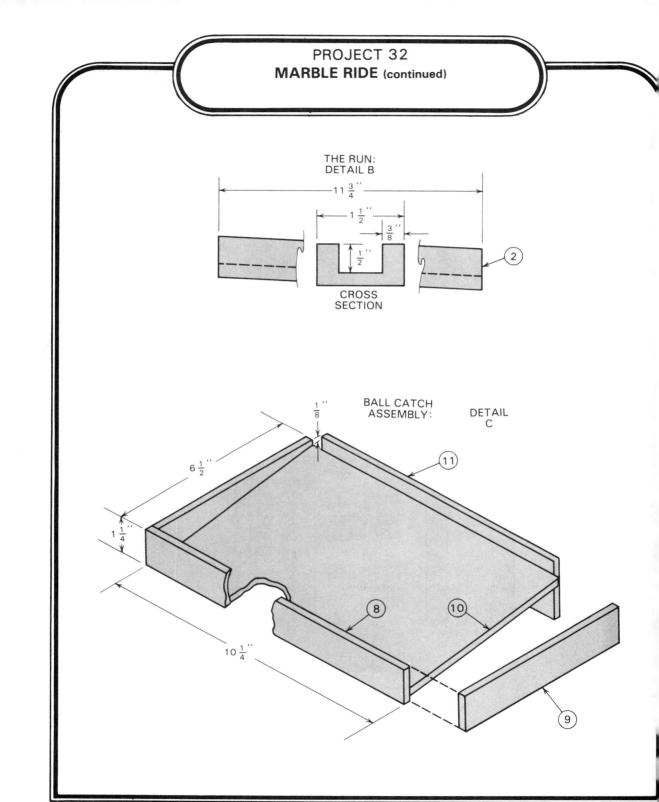

BALL CATCH
ASSEMBLY:

DETAIL
C

$\frac{1}{8}''$

$6\frac{1}{2}''$

⑪ 11

$1\frac{1}{4}''$

⑧ 8

⑩ 10

$10\frac{1}{4}''$

⑨ 9

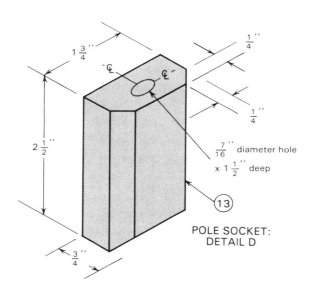

$1\frac{3}{4}''$

$\frac{1}{4}''$

$\frac{1}{4}''$

℄

℄

$2\frac{1}{2}''$

$\frac{7}{16}''$ diameter hole
x $1\frac{1}{2}''$ deep

(13)

POLE SOCKET:
DETAIL D

$\frac{3}{4}''$

FLAGS:
DETAIL E

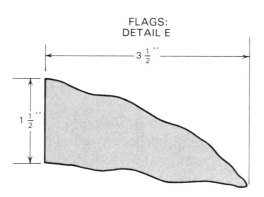

$3\frac{1}{2}''$

$1\frac{1}{2}''$

the part. Step 4 (of Detail A) shows how the marbles travel through the returns after the *runs* have been installed.

Make the *runs* to the shape and size shown in Detail B. Here it may be more convenient to form the $\frac{1}{2} \times \frac{3}{4}$-inch-wide groove in a piece of stock that is long enough to be cut up into the number of runs that are required. The runs can also be made by gluing and nailing $\frac{3}{8} \times \frac{1}{2}$-inch-wide side pieces to a $\frac{1}{4} \times 1\frac{1}{2}$-inch-wide base.

The ends of the runs and the bottom of the returns are angled $2\frac{1}{2}$ degrees. This is easy to do on a disc or belt sander and can be done by hand if you work with coarse sandpaper or files. In either case, form the angle on one part and then use the piece as a pattern to mark the others.

Start assembly by using glue and 1-inch brads to join the ends (part no. 5) to the backs (part 6). Make a U-shaped jig by tack-nailing three strips of wood to a bench-top. The legs of the U must be parallel, 90 degrees to the base, with inside surfaces $13\frac{3}{4}$ inches apart. Place the L-shaped assemblies you have (parts 5 and 6), open end up, against the legs of the U and with one end snug against the base. You can use small C-clamps or spring clamps to keep the two assemblies in place.

Add the returns and the runs in this fashion, applying glue to mating surfaces before installing each piece. First install the top left return, then the first run, then the top right return and the second run, and so on. The idea is to eliminate the need for clamping by making the runs just long enough so they must be forced into position. The bottom of the entry hole in the returns must align with the bottom of the groove in the runs. The procedure is not complicated if you take it step-by-step. If you wish, you can do a dry run: Before doing the final assembly, put parts together without glue in order to check positions.

The short *entry* and *exit* runs are attached with glue and reinforced with $\frac{5}{8}$-inch brads that are driven at a slant (toe-nailed) through the top edges of the runs into the returns.

The final step, while the parts are still in the jig, is to add the two *fronts* (part 7) with glue and a few 1-inch brads located to avoid the holes in the returns or the grooves in the runs.

The *ball-catch* assembly is shown in Detail C. This can be assembled as

project 32
Marble Ride

MATERIALS LIST

Part No.	Name	Pieces	Size	Material
1	returns	6	$1\frac{1}{2} \times 1\frac{1}{2} \times 3''$	lumber
2	runs*	5	$\frac{3}{4} \times 1\frac{1}{2} \times 12\frac{1}{2}''$	"
3	entry run	1	$\frac{3}{4} \times 1\frac{1}{2} \times 3\frac{1}{2}''$	"
4	exit run	1	$\frac{3}{4} \times 1\frac{1}{2} \times 6''$	"
5	ends	2	$\frac{1}{4} \times 2\frac{1}{2} \times 18\frac{1}{2}''$	plywood
6	backs	2	$\frac{1}{2} \times 2 \times 18\frac{1}{2}''$	plywood or lumber
7	front	2	$\frac{1}{2} \times 1\frac{1}{2} \times 18\frac{1}{2}''$	"
Ball Catch Parts				
8	front	1	$\frac{1}{4} \times 1\frac{1}{4} \times 10\frac{1}{4}''$	plywood
9	sides	2	$\frac{1}{4} \times 1\frac{1}{4} \times 6\frac{1}{4}''$	"
10	bottom*	1	$\frac{1}{4} \times 7 \times 9\frac{3}{4}''$	"
11	back	1	$\frac{1}{4} \times 2 \times 9\frac{1}{4}''$	"
12	filler block	1	$\frac{3}{4} \times 1\frac{1}{2} \times 1\frac{1}{2}''$	lumber
13	pole socket	2	$\frac{3}{4} \times 1\frac{3}{4} \times 2\frac{1}{2}''$	"
14	flag poles	2	$\frac{3}{8} \times 11''$	dowel
15	banner	1	$\frac{1}{4} \times 2\frac{1}{2} \times 13''$	plywood

*Length of runs and the width of ball catch bottom are listed oversize so they may be fitted on assembly.

a unit, but be sure the total width will match the distance between the inside edges of the front pieces (part 7).

The *pole sockets,* which are glued to the unit, are shaped as shown in Detail D. Make the *flag poles* from $\frac{3}{8}$-inch dowel and the *banner,* shaped as shown in the main drawing, from $\frac{1}{4}$-inch plywood. The *flags* (Detail E) are cut from heavy construction paper and attached to the poles with cement or glue.

Marble Roller Coaster

The action of the Marble Roller Coaster is different from that of the Marble Ride. Here, the balls make quick U-turns at the end of each run, and they are always visible. At the end of travel, the balls fall through an opening in the bottom basin and are collected in a "barrel."

Start construction by making the *runs* and the *returns*. The runs are made from strips of $\frac{3}{4} \times 1\frac{1}{2}$-inch stock that are V-cut to the dimensions shown in Detail C in the drawing. This V shape can be either cut in a long piece that you then cut off into individual parts, or in pieces that are precut to

The Marble Roller Coaster was finished in natural tones and decorated with strips of self-adhesive aluminum tape. The titles were done on a label maker, but you can substitute self-adhesive letters from stationery stores.

project 33
Marble Roller Coaster
MATERIALS LIST

Part No.	Name	Pieces	Size	Material
1	returns*	8	$\frac{3}{4} \times 2 \times 3\frac{1}{2}''$	lumber
2	runs**	8	$\frac{3}{4} \times 1\frac{1}{2} \times 12\frac{1}{2}''$	"
3	ends	2	$\frac{5}{8} \times 3\frac{1}{2} \times 18\frac{3}{4}''$	lumber or plywood
4	sides	4	$\frac{1}{4} \times 2\frac{5}{8} \times 15\frac{1}{2}''$	"
5	bottom	1	$\frac{3}{4} \times 3\frac{1}{2} \times 15\frac{3}{4}''$	lumber
6	height block	1	$\frac{3}{4} \times 1\frac{1}{2} \times 3\frac{1}{2}''$	"
7	ball return	1	made from mailing tube (see text)	
8	ball guides	2	$\frac{1}{2} \times \frac{3}{4} \times 14\frac{1}{4}''$	lumber
9	closure	2	$\frac{3}{4} \times 1\frac{1}{2} \times 12''$	"
10	backstops	7	$\frac{3}{4} \times 2 \times 3\frac{1}{2}''$	"
Parts for Marble Barrel				
11	barrel	1	3" dia. $\times$ 3"	mailing tube
12	barrel bottom	1	cut to suit	plywood or lumber

*See text for actual size.
**Length is oversize so parts may be fitted on assembly.

length. In either case, cut the pieces longer than necessary so they can be trimmed to exact length on assembly.

The returns, shown in Detail A, require semicircular V-grooves that will mate with the V-grooves in the runs. The best way to make them is to use the pivot-cutting technique that is shown in Detail B and in the photograph. The pivot block is a scrap piece of wood with a nail through it. The block is clamped to the tool's table so the distance from the nail to the point of the router bit equals $\frac{7}{8}$ inch. Then the stock is mounted as shown in the photo and rotated against the cutter's direction of rotation. Use a high speed

The setup used to form the circular V-grooves for the returns. The cutter is a 45-degree V-groove router bit. The grooves will be smoothest if you get to the full depth of cut by making repeat passes.

and achieve full depth-of-cut by making repeat passes, cutting about $\frac{1}{8}$ inch deep for each.

Start with a piece of wood that is well oversize so that you can work without getting your fingers close to the cutter. After the V-groove is formed, cut the entire piece $3\frac{1}{2}$ inches wide and 4 inches long. Be sure the circular groove and the work have a common centerline. Slice the part in half and you have two returns. This will make the piece a bit smaller than the 2-inch dimension called for, but the change will not be critical.

Next, make a U-shaped jig by tack-nailing strips of wood to a bench-top. The legs of the U must be parallel, with inside edges 17 inches apart. Make the *ends* (part 3) and the *sides* (part 4) and assemble one side—the back one —to each end with glue and 1-inch brads. Put these subassemblies in the jig, back surface down, and with top edges butting against the base of the U.

Put the top left and the top right returns in approximate position, and then use the top run to determine the exact position of the returns. Repeat this procedure with a second run and a second return, and this will reveal the distance the returns should be spaced. Now, after carefully marking their positions, you can install all the returns by using glue and short brads driven through the sides that have been installed. Add the remaining two sides, again using glue and short brads, and then return the parts to the jig.

Now it's time to install the runs. Cut them overlong—just enough so they must be forced into position between the returns. Coat mating surfaces with glue, put the runs in place, and then allow the assembly to sit until the glue is dry. The free end of the bottom run can be held against the side piece with a small clamp after the mating areas have been coated with glue.

Make the ball-catch as a subassembly as shown in Detail E. First shape the bottom (part 5), and check it on assembly to be sure it will fit correctly. Add the remaining parts and install the unit with glue and 1-inch brads that you drive through the side pieces. The ball return (part 7) is cut from a 3-inch mailing tube and is connected to the height block with glue and small nails. Use glue and 4d finishing nails to attach the closure pieces (part 9).

The final step is to make the backstops that are shown in Detail D. A quick procedure is to use a hole saw or fly cutter to form a $2\frac{1}{2}$-inch-diameter

The marble barrel was painted white and then decorated with colorful, self-adhesive tapes and stars.

hole in a piece of suitable-size stock, and then saw the piece in half to get two parts. Round off the front corners as the drawing shows, then coat the edges and the bottom of the pieces with glue and slip them into place. Press them by hand to make good contact, and then let them sit until the glue is dry.

Detail F shows how the Marble Barrel is made. Use the section of mailing tube as a template to mark the size of the disc used as a base. Install the disc with glue and with four 2d nails spaced 90 degrees apart.

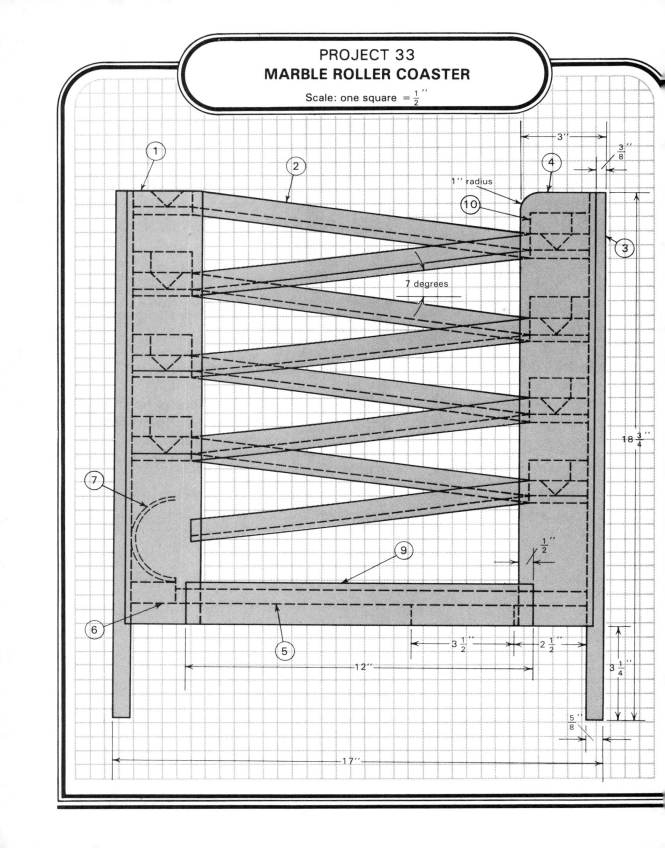

PROJECT 33
MARBLE ROLLER COASTER
Scale: one square $= \frac{1}{2}''$

3''

$\frac{3}{8}''$

1'' radius

7 degrees

$18\frac{3}{4}''$

$\frac{1}{2}''$

$3\frac{1}{2}''$

$2\frac{1}{2}''$

12''

$3\frac{1}{4}''$

$\frac{5}{8}''$

17''

PROJECT 33
MARBLE ROLLER COASTER (continued)
Scale: one square = $\frac{1}{2}$″

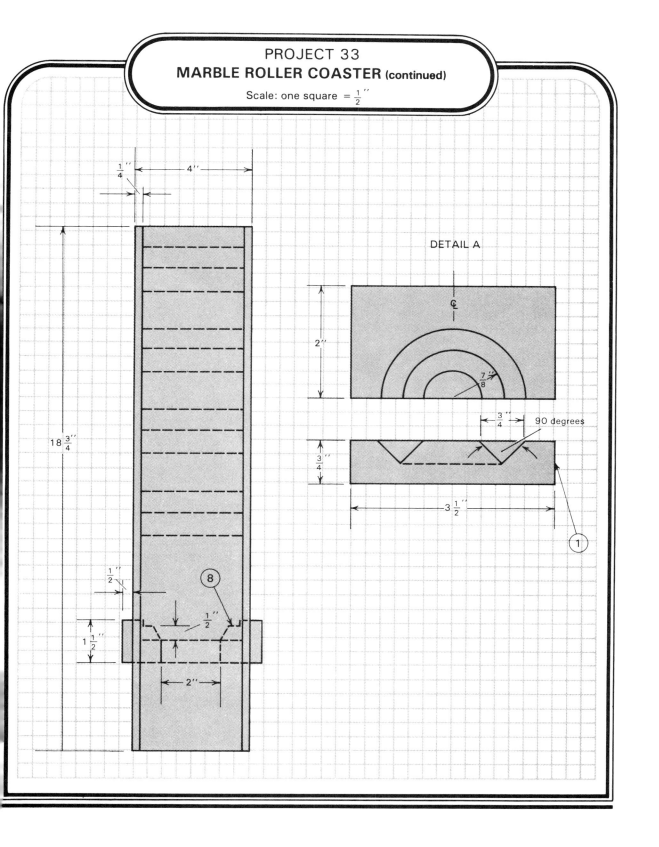

DETAIL A

$\frac{1}{4}$″ 4″

$18\frac{3}{4}$″

$\frac{1}{2}$″

$\frac{1}{2}$″

8

$1\frac{1}{2}$″

2″

2″

C

$\frac{7}{8}$″

$\frac{3}{4}$″ 90 degrees

$\frac{3}{4}$″

$3\frac{1}{2}$″

1

PROJECT 33

MARBLE ROLLER COASTER (continued)

DETAIL B

45 degrees
V router bit
shown oversize
nail
pivot
Pivot block is
clamped to
table.

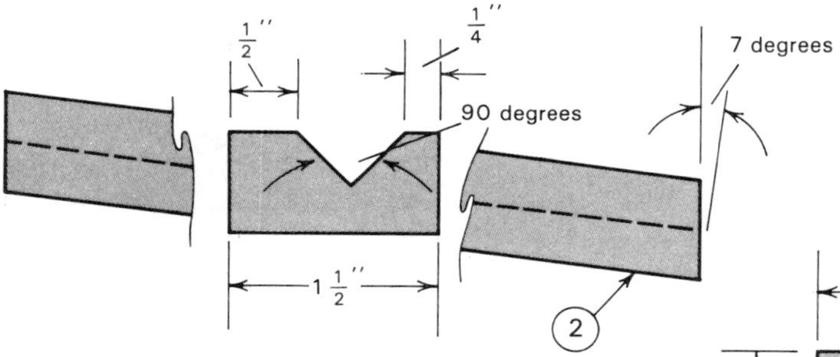

1/2"
1/4"
7 degrees
90 degrees
1 1/2"
2

DETAIL C
CROSS SECTION

DETAIL D

3 1/2"
℄
2"
1 1/4"
3/8" radius
3/4"
10

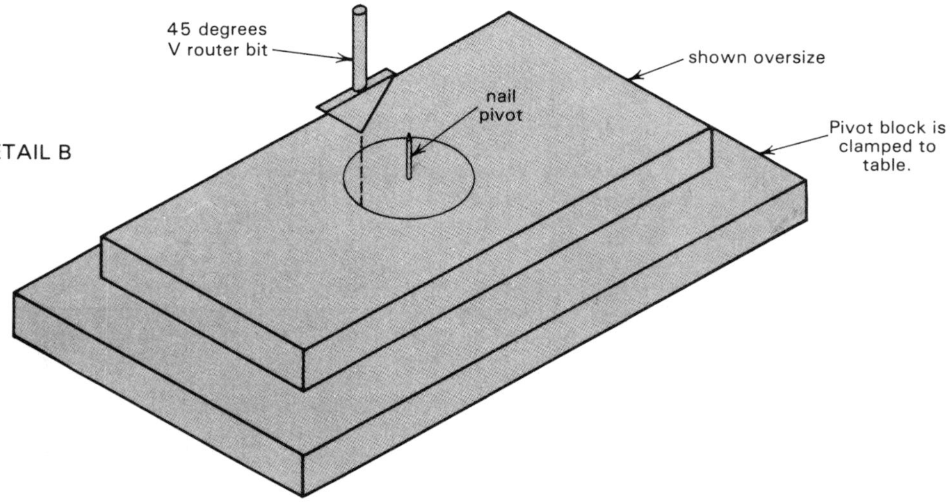

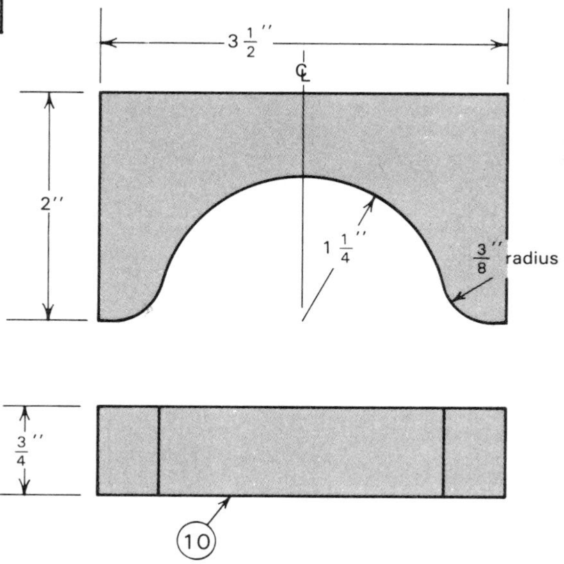

DETAIL E

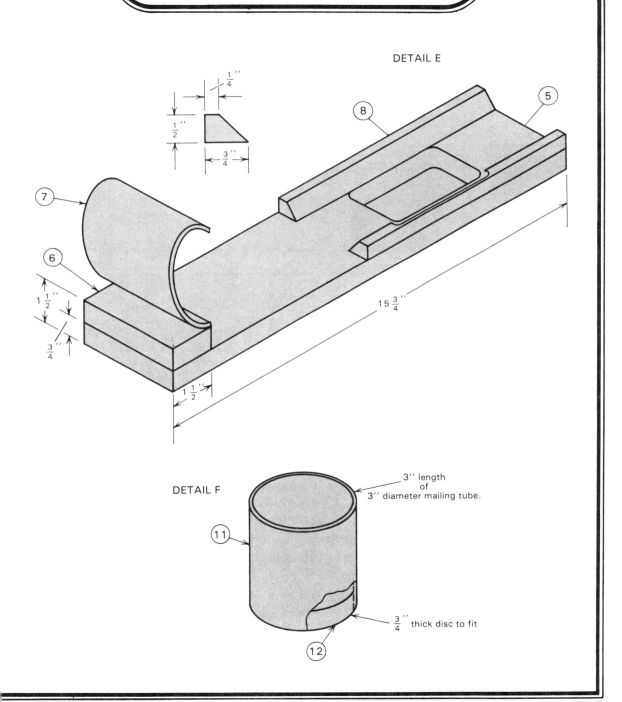

$\frac{1}{4}''$

$\frac{1}{2}''$

$\frac{3}{4}''$

8

5

7

6

$1\frac{1}{2}''$

$\frac{3}{4}''$

$1\frac{1}{2}''$

$15\frac{3}{4}''$

DETAIL F

3'' length
of
3'' diameter mailing tube.

11

$\frac{3}{4}''$ thick disc to fit

12

WAGONS

Toy-Tote Wagon

Kids like to be transported, but they also enjoy being the transporter. The Toy-Tote Wagon is maneuverable and sized especially to suit the stuffed toys and animals a child is likely to have. Maybe it's a way for youngsters to emulate the parent who pulls them about in a large wagon.

Make the bed first, and then add the front and rear pieces, securing them with glue and 6d box nails. Form the sides using $\frac{1}{4}$-inch hardboard or plywood, and put them in place with glue and 4d box nails. If you use hardboard, drill small pilot holes for the nails so that they will be less likely to bend when you hammer them.

Make and attach the axle blocks, using a length of $\frac{1}{2}$-inch dowel as a gauge so the two pieces will be correctly aligned. The piece for the yoke, sized $\frac{3}{4} \times 3\frac{1}{2} \times 11$ inches to begin with, is shaped at the front as shown

222

All parts have a natural finish. The stripes and stars are self-adhesive products. The turtle was cut from children's-room wallpaper.

Proud owner of new transport system. The Toy-Tote Wagon proved to be a big deal for David. It was his to load and pull indoors and outdoors.

in the detail drawing. Attach it to the underside of the bed with glue and the screws called for in the drawing.

Next, make the rear axle and wheels. The length of the axle should be just enough to leave about an $\frac{1}{8}$-inch recess in the wheel holes so that the wood button, which serves as a hub, can be glued into place. Coat the ends of the axle with glue before pressing the wheels into place. If it is easier for you to eliminate the wood button, let the axle ends come flush with the outside surfaces of the wheels and then glue on a 1-inch-diameter disc of $\frac{1}{8}$- or $\frac{1}{4}$-inch-thick hardboard or plywood. The wheel "tires" (part 8) are strips cut from sheet cork which are put in place with contact cement or glue. If you use glue, hold the tires in place with a heavy rubber band until the glue dries.

The front wheel is a swivel-type plate caster with a 2-inch-diameter plastic wheel. Attach the caster to the underside of the yoke with the screws that are supplied with the unit.

Cut the handle to size and drill a hole at the bottom end for the axle and one at the top end for the grip. The hole at the top must provide a tight fit for the grip. At the bottom, the axle must fit tightly in the yoke, but be loose in the handle.

project 34
Toy-Tote Wagon

MATERIALS LIST

Part No.	Name	Pieces	Size	Material
1	bed	1	$\frac{3}{4} \times 12 \times 16\frac{1}{2}''$	plywood
2	front	1	$\frac{3}{4} \times 5 \times 12''$	"
3	rear	1	$\frac{3}{4} \times 4 \times 12''$	"
4	sides	2	$\frac{1}{4} \times 7\frac{1}{2} \times 18''$	hardboard
5	axle blocks	2	$1\frac{1}{8} \times 1\frac{1}{2} \times 3\frac{1}{2}''$	lumber
6	yoke	1	$\frac{3}{4} \times 3\frac{1}{2} \times 11''$	"
7	rear wheels	2	$\frac{1}{2} \times 5\frac{1}{4}''$ diameter	plywood (or lumber)
8	wheel "tires"	2	$\frac{1}{8} \times \frac{1}{2} \times 18''$	cut from sheet cork
9	axle	1	$\frac{1}{2} \times 13\frac{1}{2}''$	dowel
10	hubs	2	$\frac{1}{2}''$	wood buttons
11	handle	1	$\frac{3}{4} \times 1\frac{1}{4} \times 22''$	lumber
12	handle grip	1	$\frac{3}{8} \times 4''$	dowel
13	handle axle	1	$\frac{3}{8} \times 4''$	"
14	front wheel	1	$2''$	swivel type plate caster with plastic wheel

Hole through axle blocks $= \frac{9}{16}''$
Hole through rear wheels $= \frac{1}{2}''$
Hole through yoke $= \frac{3}{8}''$
Hole through handle $= \frac{7}{16}''$
Hole for handle grip $= \frac{3}{8}''$

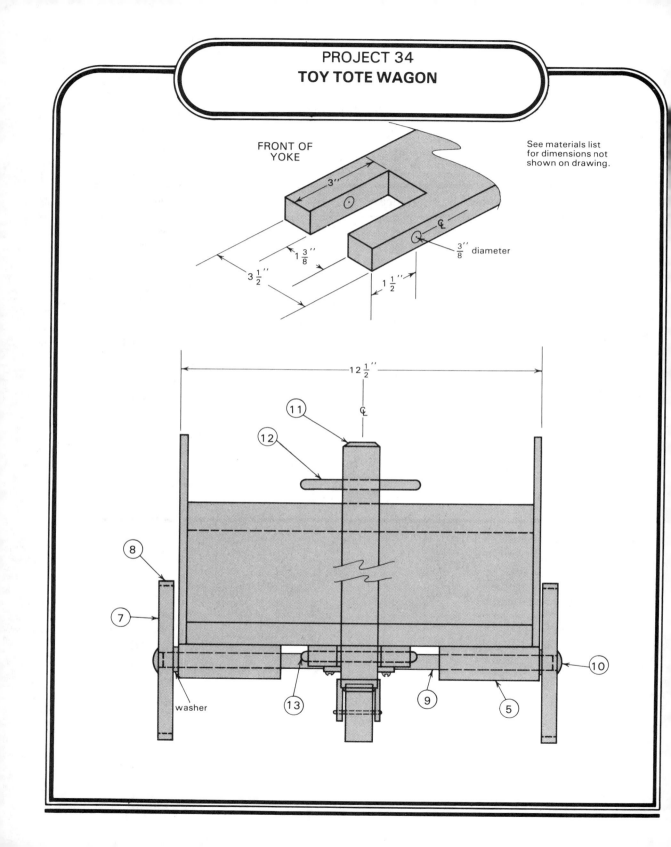

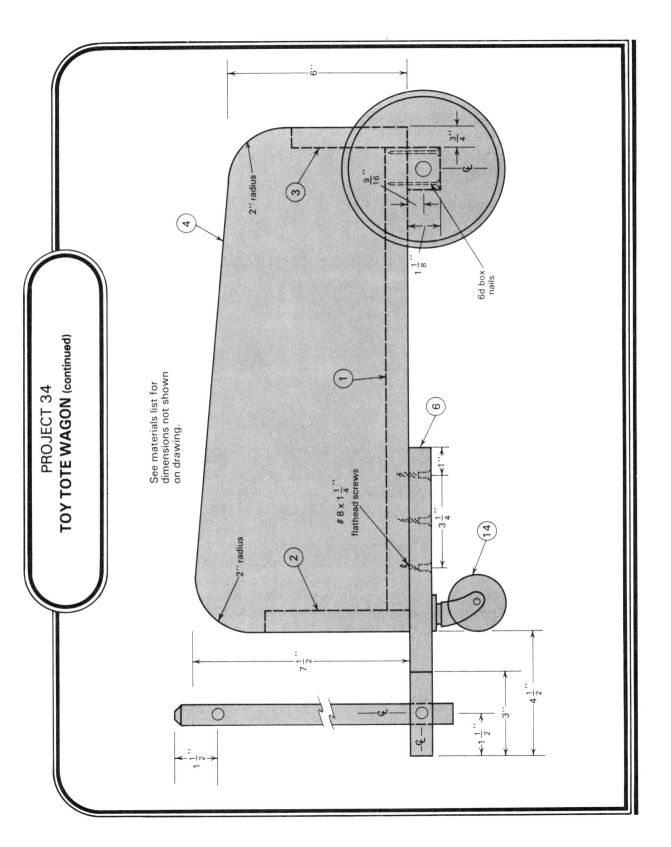

PROJECT 34
TOY TOTE WAGON (continued)

See materials list for dimensions not shown on drawing.

2'' radius

6d box nails

#8 x 1 1/4'' flathead screws

2'' radius

2'' radius

Express Wagon

Start the project by making the bed—a piece of $\frac{3}{4}$-inch-thick, cabinet-grade plywood that will measure 16 inches wide by $24\frac{1}{4}$ inches long. Mark the locations of the screws that will be driven through the bed to secure the rear axle block and the front cleat. For now, drill small pilot holes at these points. They will be used to locate matching holes required in the axle block and cleat.

Cut the front and the back pieces to size, and after forming the rabbet in the bottom edges, attach them to the bed with glue and 4d box nails.

Cut the material that is required for the front and rear side pieces (parts 4 and 5). Mark these so you can identify which surface of each piece must face the inside of the wagon. This is important, because the direction of the rabbet cuts and dadoes must face the proper way when the parts are

The removable sides, bed, front, and rear pieces are plywood. All other parts are lumber. Finishing was done with coats of sealer. The wheel washers were rimmed with red tape.

installed. The rabbet cuts along the bottom edge of each piece should be $\frac{3}{4}$ inch deep by 1 inch wide. The grooves that are needed for the removable sides are $\frac{3}{4}$ inch deep and $\frac{5}{8}$ inch wide. If you are working on a table saw,

The steering post and yoke arrangement. A lock nut on the handle bolt provides security while still allowing the handle to pivot.

be aware, because the pieces are relatively small. The safest way to form the grooves is with a tenoning jig. If you lack such an accessory, do the cutting on pieces that are large enough to be safely handled. Then saw the pieces to final size.

Shape the front pieces as shown in the drawing, round off the inside corner of the rear pieces, and then attach the parts to the bed with glue and 5d or 6d nails. Make and install the front and rear posts using glue and 5d finishing nails.

Next, cut two 14-inch lengths of $1\frac{1}{2} \times 3\frac{1}{2}$-inch stock, and in each of them form the V-groove shown in Detail A. Saw one of them so it will produce both the front cleat (part 10) and the front axle block (part 12). The remaining piece, shaped as shown in Detail B, will be the rear axle block (part 9). Bore the $\frac{3}{4}$-inch-diameter hole that will be used for the steering post (Detail

project 35

Express Wagon

MATERIALS LIST

Part No.	Name	Pieces	Size	Material
1	bed	1	$\frac{3}{4} \times 16 \times 24\frac{1}{4}''$	plywood
2	front	1	$\frac{3}{4} \times 5\frac{1}{2} \times 16''$	plywood or lumber
3	back	1	$\frac{3}{4} \times 4\frac{1}{4} \times 16''$	"
4	sides (front)	2	$1\frac{1}{2} \times 5\frac{1}{2} \times 7''$	lumber
5	sides (rear)	2	$1\frac{1}{2} \times 4\frac{1}{4} \times 5''$	"
6	front posts	2	$\frac{5}{8} \times \frac{7}{8} \times 7''$	"
7	rear posts	2	$\frac{5}{8} \times \frac{7}{8} \times 5''$	"
8	removable sides	2	$\frac{1}{2} \times 4\frac{1}{2} \times 12\frac{1}{2}''$	plywood
9	rear axle block	1	$1\frac{1}{2} \times 3\frac{1}{2} \times 14''$	lumber
10	front cleat	1	$1\frac{1}{2} \times 1\frac{1}{2} \times 14''$	"
11	washer	1	$\frac{1}{4} \times 3''$ dia.	temp. hardboard
12	front axle block	1	$1\frac{1}{2} \times 1\frac{3}{4} \times 14''$	lumber
13	rear axle	1	$\frac{3}{4} \times 20''$	dowel
14	front axles	2	$\frac{3}{4} \times 8\frac{1}{2}''$	"
15	washers	8	$\frac{1}{4} \times 2''$ dia.	temp. hardboard
16	wheels	4	$1\frac{1}{2} \times 5\frac{1}{4}''$ dia.	lumber
17	wheel locks	4	$\frac{1}{4} \times 2''$	dowel
18	steering post	1	$\frac{3}{4} \times 5\frac{1}{2}''$	"
19	steering post retainer	1	$1\frac{1}{4} \times 1\frac{1}{4} \times 1\frac{1}{2}''$	lumber
20	yoke	1	$1\frac{1}{2} \times 7 \times 7''$	"
21	handle	1	$\frac{3}{4} \times 22''$	aluminum tube
22	handle grip	1	$1 \times 2 \times 7''$	lumber
23	handle bolt	1	$\frac{3}{8} \times 2\frac{1}{2}''$	bolt w/two washers and a *lock* nut

C) in the front cleat, and then proceed to attach cleat and rear axle to the bed. Put them temporarily into position and bore screw-starting holes by drilling through the pilot holes you already have in the bed. Enlarge the pilot holes to $\frac{3}{16}$ or $\frac{7}{32}$ inch, coat mating surfaces with glue, and then drive home the 2-inch flathead screws.

Bore the $\frac{3}{4}$-inch-diameter hole required for the steering post through the front axle block, then cut to length and attach the two front axles and the single rear one (Detail A). Do not, at this point, drill the wheel-lock holes through the axles.

The steering-post arrangement is shown in Detail C. Make the antifriction washer (part 11) and the retainer (part 19) and assemble the unit as illustrated. Attach the steering post (in the hole in the front cleat) with glue and two #6 1-inch screws. Add the washer and the axle block, then the metal washer, and finally the retainer—which you only attach with screws.

The yoke is shaped as shown in Detail D. The easiest way to form the notch is to first bore a 1-inch hole with its center $3\frac{1}{2}$ inches from the yoke's end. Then saw out the waste piece. Attach the yoke to the front axle block with glue and four #10 $1\frac{3}{4}$-inch screws.

Cut the wheel washers (part 15) by working as if you were making small wheels. Make the four wheels and then add washers and wheels to the axles. Drill holes through the axles for the $\frac{1}{4}$-inch dowels used as wheel locks. Locate the locks so that they allow just enough clearance for the wheels to turn. Detail E shows an optional wheel arrangement. The bushing can be aluminum tubing that has a $\frac{3}{4}$-inch inside diameter. Size the hole through the wheel so that the bushing can be a press fit. If the wheel doesn't turn freely on the axle, work with fine sandpaper and dress the axle to suit.

Final steps are to make the removable sides and the handle assembly. Bore the hole in the handle grip before you cut the part to outline shape. Attach it to the handle with two #6 1-inch screws. The bolt that passes through the yoke and the handle is secured with a *lock nut.* Lock nuts are sold in auto-supply stores if not available at your hardware store. Lock nuts will stay put at any point on the bolt.

One more point: The handle length in the drawing is okay for youngsters, but too short when adults are pulling the wagon. An extra, longer handle will prevent back cricks.

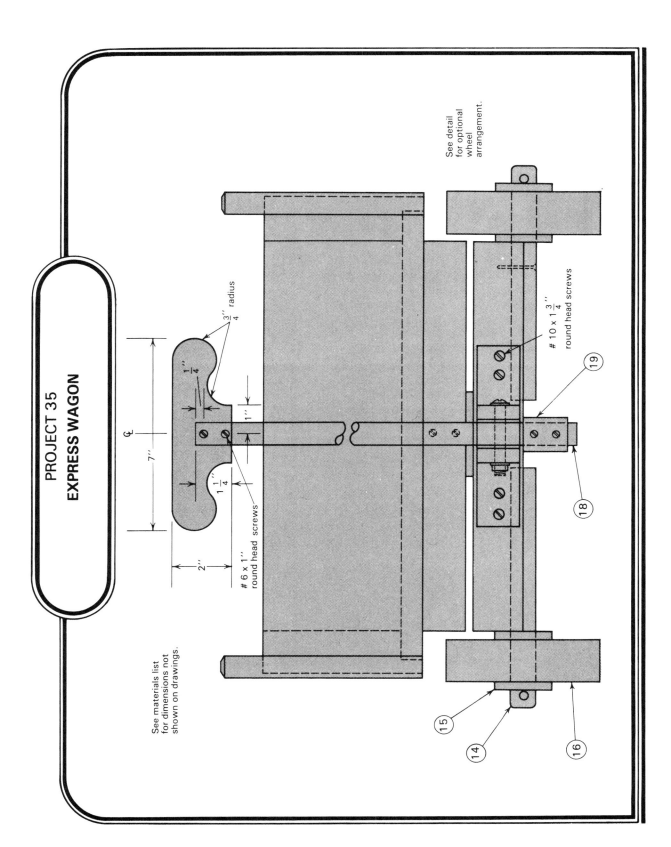

PROJECT 35
EXPRESS WAGON

See detail for optional wheel arrangement.

3/4″ radius

1/4″

1″

7″

1 1/4″

2″

#6 x 1″ round head screws

#10 x 1 3/4″ round head screws

See materials list for dimensions not shown on drawings.

(14)
(15)
(16)
(18)
(19)

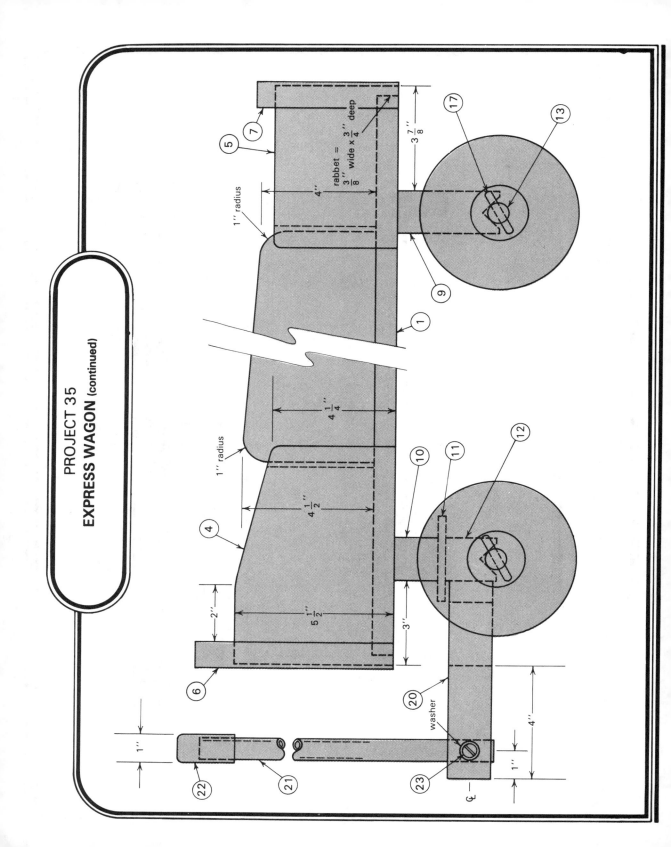

PROJECT 35
EXPRESS WAGON (continued)

PROJECT 35
EXPRESS WAGON (continued)

TOP VIEW

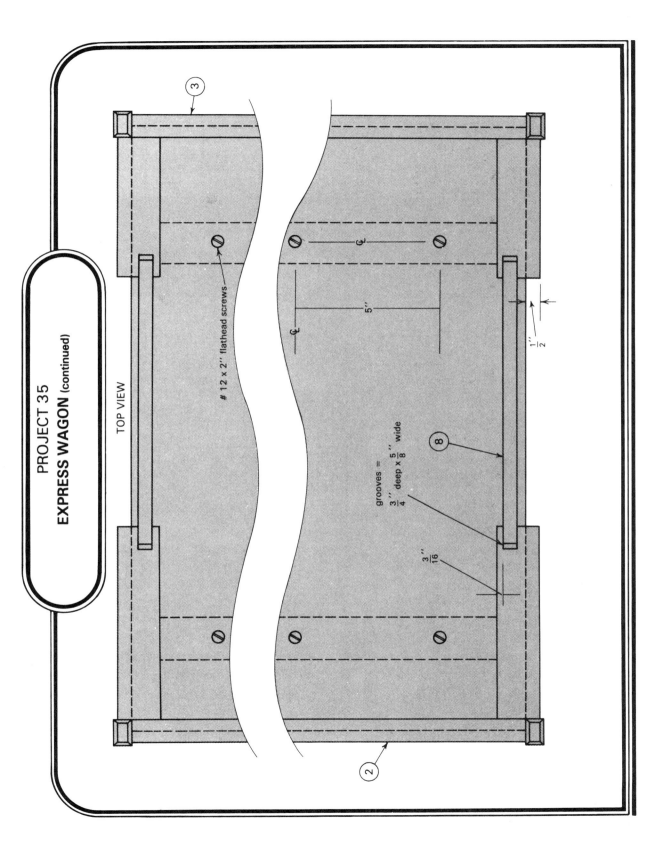

12 x 2'' flathead screws

grooves =
$\frac{3}{4}$'' deep x $\frac{5}{8}$'' wide

$\frac{3}{16}$''

5''

$\frac{1}{2}$''

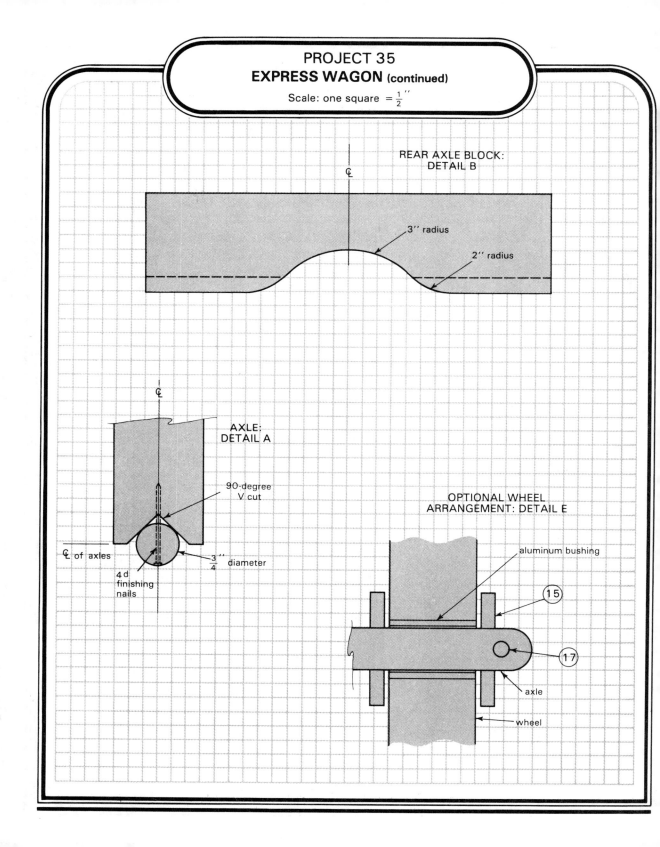

PROJECT 35
EXPRESS WAGON (continued)

Scale: one square = $\frac{1}{2}$"

REAR AXLE BLOCK:
DETAIL B

3" radius

2" radius

AXLE:
DETAIL A

90-degree
V cut

OPTIONAL WHEEL
ARRANGEMENT: DETAIL E

aluminum bushing

Ȼ of axles

$\frac{3}{4}$" diameter

4 d
finishing
nails

(15)

(17)

axle

wheel

PROJECT 35
EXPRESS WAGON (continued)

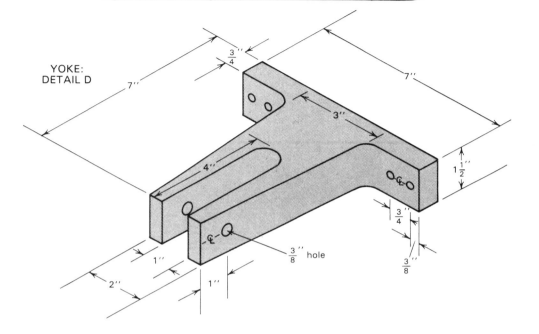

YOKE:
DETAIL D

$\frac{3}{4}''$

7''

7''

3''

4''

$1\frac{1}{2}''$

$\frac{3}{4}''$

$\frac{3}{8}''$

$\frac{3}{8}''$ hole

1''

2''

1''

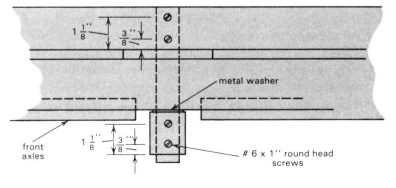

STEERING POST:
DETAIL C

$1\frac{1}{8}''$ $\frac{3}{8}''$

metal washer

front axles

$1\frac{1}{8}''$ $\frac{3}{8}''$

6 x 1'' round head screws

RIDING TOYS

Kiddie Car

Kids like to be mobile—whether they're on wheels, straddling a project and pretending to ride, or just rocking. These are major reasons why the projects in this section will always be popular. The first two are traditional. The third, the No-Gas Car, is the "ultimate driving machine" for the youngster who hasn't yet cast his eyes on a full-size bike and is far from thoughts of a motorcycle or automobile.

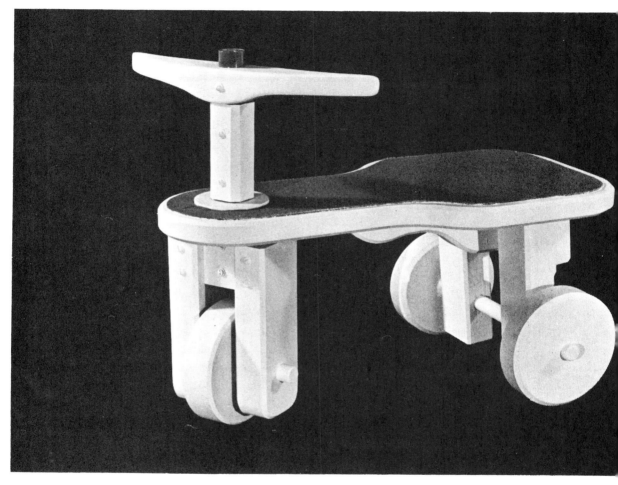

The Kiddie Car was finished by first applying a coat of sealer and then a coat of yellow paint. The pad on the seat is a piece of indoor-outdoor carpeting. It can be attached with glue, contact cement, or even with strips of heavy double-face tape.

project 36
Kiddie Car

MATERIALS LIST

Part No.	Name	Pieces	Size	Material
1	seat	1	$1 \times 10 \times 20''$	plywood or lumber
2	wheel posts (rear)	2	$1\frac{1}{2} \times 2\frac{1}{2} \times 8''$	lumber
3	rear support	1	$1\frac{1}{2} \times 2\frac{3}{8} \times 7\frac{1}{2}''$	"
4	wheel posts (front)	2	$1\frac{1}{2} \times 2\frac{1}{2} \times 7\frac{3}{4}''$	"
5	front support	1	$1\frac{1}{2} \times 2\frac{1}{4} \times 5''$	"
6	brace	1	$1\frac{1}{2} \times 2\frac{3}{8} \times 8\frac{1}{4}''$	"
7	steering column	1	$1\frac{1}{2} \times 1\frac{1}{2} \times 4''$	"
8	steering post	1	$\frac{3}{4} \times 9\frac{1}{4}''$	aluminum tube
9	washers	2	$\frac{1}{4} \times 3''$ dia.	temp. hardboard
10	wheels	3	$1\frac{1}{2} \times 5\frac{1}{2}''$ dia.	lumber
11	washers	2	$\frac{1}{4} \times 2''$ dia.	temp. hardboard
12	washers	2	$\frac{1}{4} \times 1\frac{1}{2}''$ dia.	"
13	rear axle	1	$\frac{3}{4} \times 12\frac{1}{2}''$	dowel
14	front axle	1	$\frac{3}{4} \times 6\frac{1}{2}''$	"
15	handlebars	1	$1\frac{1}{2} \times 2\frac{1}{4} \times 12''$	lumber
16	plug	1	$\frac{3}{4} \times 1''$	dowel
17	cap	1	to suit	salvage

Hole through front wheel and washers = $\frac{7}{8}''$
Hole through front wheel supports = $\frac{3}{4}''$
Hole through rear wheels = $\frac{3}{4}''$
Hole through rear wheel supports and washers = $\frac{7}{8}''$

PROJECT 36
KIDDIE KAR

Scale: one square = $\frac{1}{2}$ ''

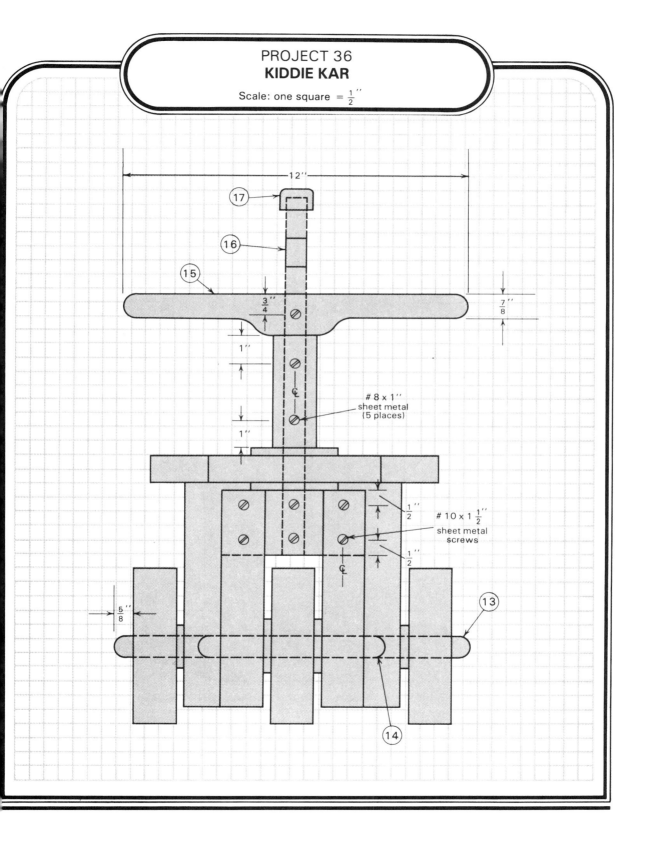

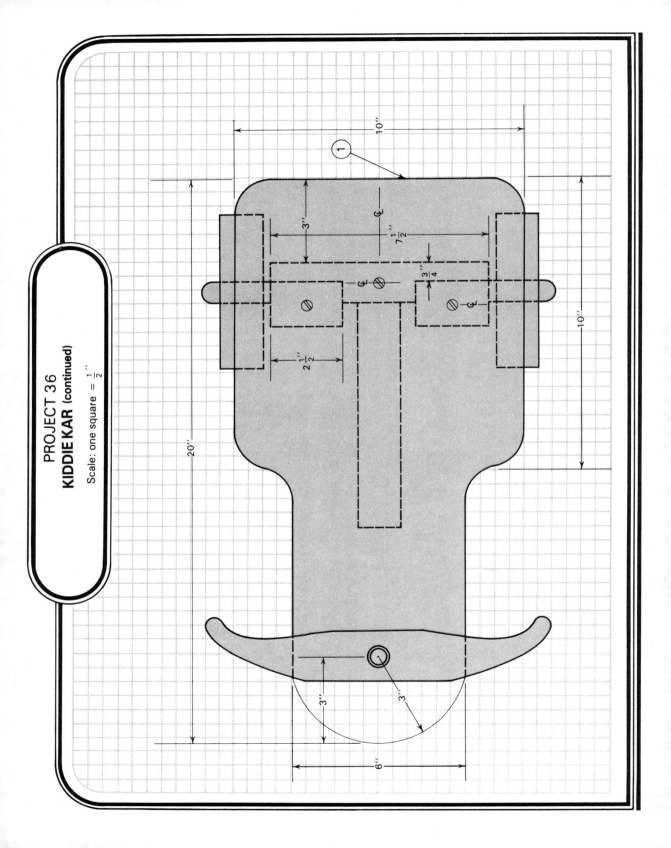

PROJECT 36
KIDDIE KAR (continued)

Scale: one square = $\frac{1}{2}$"

10"

10"

20"

1

3"

$7\frac{1}{2}$"

$\frac{3}{4}$"

$2\frac{1}{2}$"

3"

3"

6"

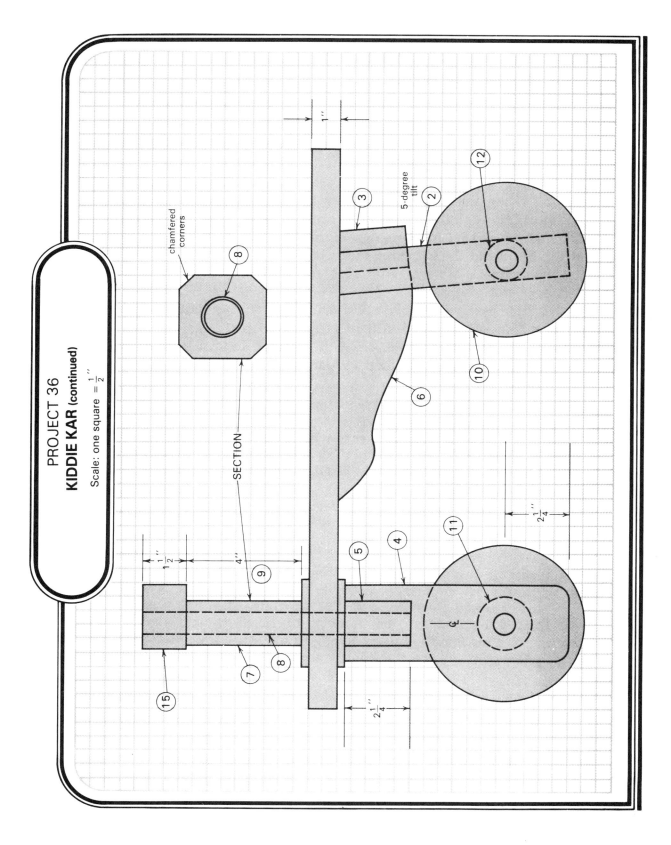

PROJECT 36
KIDDIE KAR (continued)

Scale: one square = $\frac{1}{2}$"

Start the project by shaping the seat and boring the $\frac{3}{4}$-inch steering-post hole at the front, and three pilot holes at the rear for the screws that will be used to attach the rear-wheel support assembly. Chamfer or round off the top and bottom edges of the seat and do a thorough sanding job, especially if you use plywood.

Next, make the rear posts and the support (parts 2 and 3). Bore the $\frac{7}{8}$-inch axle holes through the posts and form the rabbet cuts in the support to the dimensions shown in the top view of the drawing. Shape the top end of the posts and the top edge of the support to an angle of 5 degrees, and then assemble the pieces with glue and 6d box nails driven through the support.

Hold the assembly in place and drill through the pilot holes in the seat so you'll know where to drill the lead holes for the attachment screws. Enlarge the seat pilot holes to $\frac{3}{16}$ or $\frac{7}{32}$ inch, and after coating mating surfaces with glue, attach the parts permanently by driving home the three #12 $2\frac{1}{4}$-inch screws.

Make the assembly that consists of parts 4 and 5. Drill the $\frac{3}{4}$-inch steering-post hole through the support and the $\frac{3}{4}$-inch axle holes through the posts before assembling the pieces with glue and the #10 $1\frac{1}{2}$-inch sheet-metal screws.

Make the brace (part 6) and attach it with glue and by toenailing at the front and rear. The shape of the brace really isn't critical, so you can skip the layout that is shown and just draw something similar by working with a French curve.

Next, make the parts that compose the steering assembly—the steering post, which is a length of aluminum tubing; two washers; the steering column; and the handlebars. Assemble the parts in this order: Place the steering post in the hole that is in the front support. Add a washer and then pass the post through the hole in the seat. Add the second washer, then the steering column, and finally, the handlebars. Drill $\frac{1}{16}$-inch holes through the parts as you place them, for the #8 1-inch sheet-metal screws that are called for.

The cap, which is a recycled bottle top, adds a decorative touch, but is there primarily to seal the hole at the top of the steering post in which little fingers can sometimes get caught. Size the plug so that it will have to be forced into the post, and then glue on the cap.

Make and install the axles, wheel washers, and wheels. The rear wheels turn *with* the axle; the front wheel rotates independently.

Rocking Horse

The drawings show an easy method for tracing the arc required for the rockers. Select a piece of plywood or lumber of any width that is at least 50 inches long. Mark a centerline down the length of the material. Cut a 32-inch length of $1\frac{1}{2}$-inch-thick by 6-inch-wide lumber and clamp or tack-nail it to the first piece so that it is centered and at right angles to the centerline. Drive a nail on the centerline, 48 inches from the outside edge of the stock. Make a "compass" by tying one end of a piece of string to the nail and the other end to a pencil; the distance between pencil point and nail should be 48 inches. Keep the string taut as you move the pencil to

The Rocking Horse has a natural finish. Head details are black; short pieces of macrame material do for the mane. Use $\frac{1}{4}$- or $\frac{3}{8}$-inch-diameter smooth rope for the reins which pass through the horse's head and the upper part of the front leg.

form the arc. Reduce the length of the string by $2\frac{1}{4}$ inches and mark a second, parallel arc. While the stock is still in square form, mark the location of the holes needed for the stretchers.

If you have a band saw you can pad, or stack, the stock together so a single cutting will produce two rockers. Otherwise, saw and sand one rocker and then use it as a template to mark its twin. Drill the $\frac{5}{8}$-inch-diameter holes required for the stretchers, and then chamfer and sand outside edges so that a cross section of the pieces will look like that in Section A-A in the drawing. Cut and install the stretchers, making sure that the rockers are parallel and that the distance between outside surfaces equals 12 inches. Use glue and one 6d finishing nail to secure the stretchers.

Make the back leg, shaping the center cutout and the base notches to the dimensions that are shown in the front view of the drawing. Next, cut the piece required for the front leg, and form as the drawing shows. You can use the back leg as a template to mark the cut lines of the lower portion of the front leg.

To make the seat, first cut the material to overall size. Then form the dado in which the back leg fits and the 5-degree bevel at the front, and saw the part to shape. It's a good idea, while the seat is still free and easy to handle, to make and attach the backrest (part 7) by following the instructions shown in Detail C. At this point, you can also attach the seat to the back leg and install the brace. At first, cut the brace longer than necessary. After it is attached, cut the front end to conform to the bevel on the front edge of the seat.

Now put this assembly and the front leg temporarily in position so that you can judge exact locations. Mark the leg positions on the inside of the rockers, and make and install the glue blocks shown in Detail B. Secure them with glue and 6d finishing nails and then permanently attach the legs. Use glue and one #8 $1\frac{3}{4}$-inch screw through the legs into each glue block. Use glue and 6d finishing nails to make the bond between the front leg and the seat.

Shape the head by following the pattern shown in Detail A. Here you can do some carving if you wish—depressions for the nostrils, lips, raised eyebrows, and so on. The least you should do is round off all edges, paying particular attention to the area between mane and nose.

project 37
Rocking Horse

MATERIALS LIST

Part No.	Name	Pieces	Size	Material
1	rockers	2	$1\frac{1}{2} \times 6 \times 32''$	lumber
2	stretchers	3	$\frac{5}{8} \times 13''$	dowel
3	back leg	1	$\frac{3}{4} \times 10 \times 13''$	lumber or plywood
4	front leg	1	$\frac{3}{4} \times 10 \times 23\frac{1}{2}''$	"
5	seat	1	$1 \times 10 \times 18''$	plywood or lumber
6	brace	1	$\frac{3}{4} \times 2\frac{1}{4} \times 18''$	lumber
7	backrest	1	$1\frac{1}{2} \times 4 \times 8''$	"
8	glue blocks	4	$1 \times 1\frac{1}{2} \times 3''$	"
9	head	1	$1\frac{1}{2} \times 7 \times 9''$	"
10	screw covers	2	$\frac{1}{2}''$	wood buttons
Parts for Stirrups (Optional)				
11	sides	4	$\frac{3}{4} \times 1\frac{1}{4} \times 4''$	lumber
12	bottom rung	2	$\frac{1}{2} \times 4''$	dowel
13	top rung	2	$\frac{1}{2} \times 3\frac{1}{4}''$	"
14	strap	1	$1\frac{1}{4}''$ wide $\times$ app. $30''$	leather (or similar)

Also needed: about 36" of $\frac{3}{8}''$-diameter nylon rope
(for reins)
macrame material for mane and tail
Stretcher holes through rockers $= \frac{5}{8}''$

Hayley gets the Rocking Horse. She thought the stirrups were a good idea.

If you wish to add the stirrups, they can be made as shown in the detail drawing. The strap can be made from an old belt. It can be cut to a specific length or made adjustable by installing button snaps—which, if you don't have equipment for that kind of thing, can be done for you at a shoe repair shop.

Secure the strap to the seat with a couple of $\frac{3}{4}$-inch, panhead sheet-metal screws. Use washers under the heads.

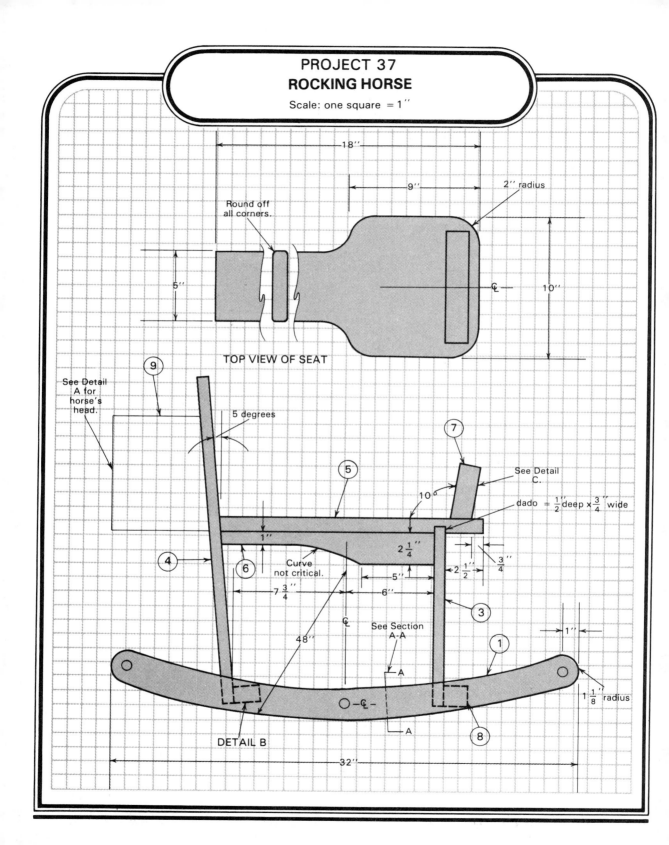

PROJECT 37
ROCKING HORSE

Scale: one square = 1''

18''

9''

2'' radius

Round off all corners.

5''

10''

₵

TOP VIEW OF SEAT

9

See Detail A for horse's head.

5 degrees

7

5

See Detail C.

10°

dado = $\frac{1}{2}$'' deep x $\frac{3}{4}$'' wide

1''

2$\frac{1}{4}$''

$\frac{3}{4}$''

4

6

Curve not critical.

2$\frac{1}{2}$''

3

7$\frac{3}{4}$''

5''

6''

₵

48''

See Section A-A

A — A

1

1''

O—₵—

1$\frac{1}{8}$'' radius

DETAIL B

A — A

8

32''

PROJECT 37
ROCKING HORSE (continued)

Scale: one square = 1″

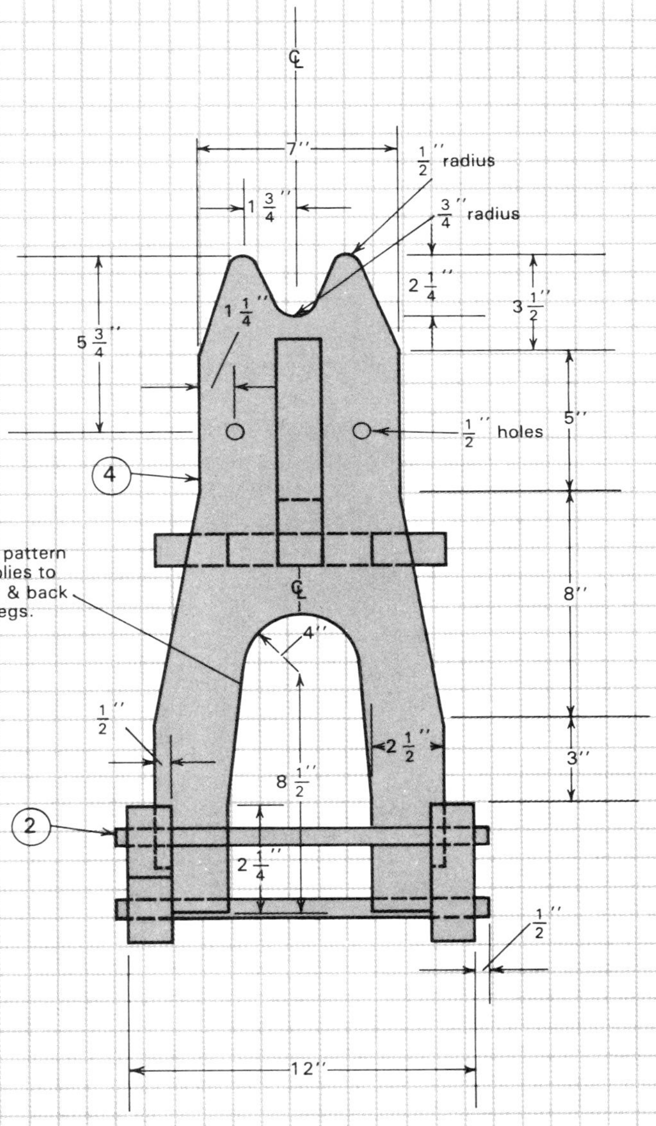

PROJECT 37
ROCKING HORSE (continued)
Scale: one square = $\frac{1}{4}$"

DETAIL A

rounded

④

⑨

1"

2$\frac{1}{2}$"

10 x 1$\frac{1}{2}$"
flathead screws

⑩

Chamfer edges.

$\frac{1}{2}$" holes

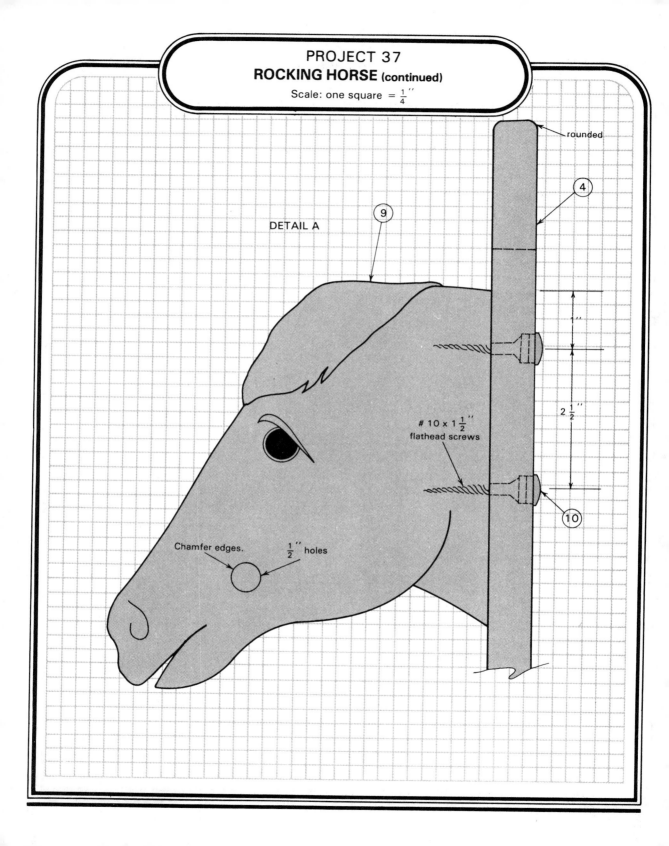

PROJECT 37
ROCKING HORSE (continued)

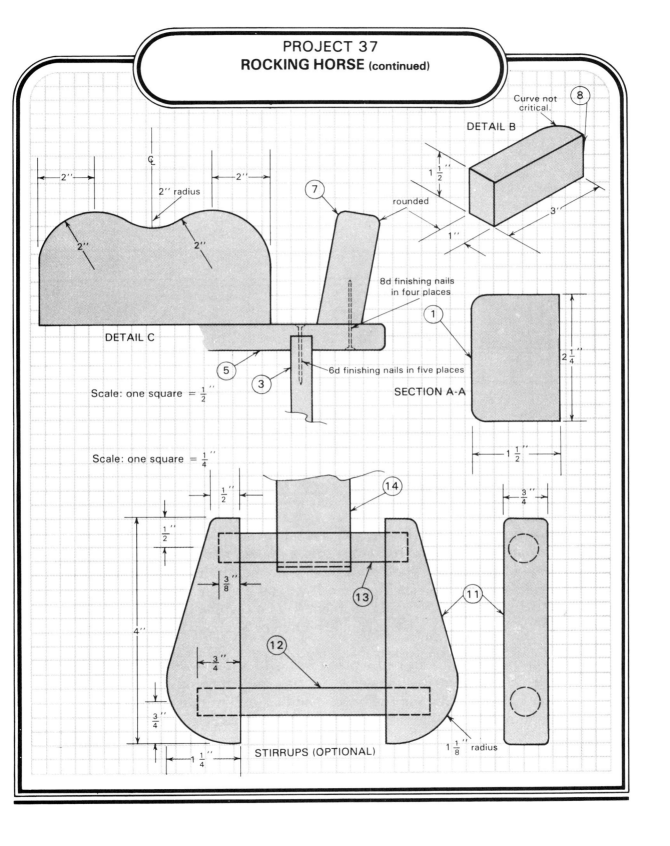

Curve not critical.

DETAIL B

1 1/2''

1''

3''

rounded

8

7

2'' radius

2''

2''

2''

2''

C

8d finishing nails in four places

6d finishing nails in five places

DETAIL C

5

3

1

2 1/4''

1 1/2''

SECTION A-A

Scale: one square = 1/2''

Scale: one square = 1/4''

14

1/2

1/2

3/8

4''

3/4

3/4

3/4

12

13

11

11

1 1/8'' radius

1 1/4

STIRRUPS (OPTIONAL)

No-Gas Car

It's not surprising that this project was one of the most popular with the test crew. It steers like the real thing, has a brake system, and because the store-bought wheels are good ones with permanently lubricated bearings, the car rolls well even on slight slopes. It will take a little time to make, but the rewards are great. Your only problem will be keeping the recipient calm until delivery time. The answer is to keep him or her busy helping with the construction.

Start the project with the bed, a piece of $\frac{3}{4} \times 16 \times 39\frac{3}{4}$-inch cabinet-grade plywood. Work from the top view of the main drawing and mark the location of all the holes and the brake-handle slot. Drill pilot holes for the screws that will secure the rear axle block and the front cleat. The two holes

The back "motor" area and steering wheel assembly of the No-Gas Car are yellow. All other parts of the car have a natural finish. The material for the steering cable was purchased in a boat supply store. Choose substantial wheels—too many have balloon-thin tires and plastic hubs.

at the front for the steering cable and the two at the rear for the brake-shoe bar can be drilled full size. To form the slot, bore two 1-inch holes with centers 3 inches apart and cut out the waste. Form the bed to its outline shape.

Next, cut two pieces of $1\frac{1}{2} \times 3\frac{1}{2}$-inch stock 18 inches long. Make the V-cut shown in Detail C in one edge of each piece and then saw one of them to produce both the front cleat (part 3) and the front axle block (part 5). Bore the $\frac{3}{4}$-inch hole (see Detail A) required for the steering post through the cleat and the front axle block, and then attach the cleat and the *rear* axle block to the bed with glue and the screws called for. You can easily locate the lead holes in the cleat and axle block by holding the parts in place and drilling through the pilot holes that are already in the bed.

The next step involves putting together the steering post assembly—shown in Detail A. The post, a $4\frac{1}{8}$-inch length of $\frac{3}{4}$-inch (outside diameter) aluminum tubing, is secured in the front cleat with two sheet-metal screws. Drill $\frac{1}{16}$-inch holes through the cleat and tube before driving the screws. Make and add the antifriction washer (part 4), then the front axle block and the metal washer, and finally the shaft collar, which is a ready-made part with its own locking set screw.

Now hacksaw $\frac{1}{2}$-inch-diameter steel rods to the lengths needed for the rear axle and the two front axles. The axles are drilled for and attached with $1\frac{1}{4}$-inch, #8 sheet-metal screws as shown in Detail C. The wheels you buy may have a different hub width than those we used; so be sure the axles extend beyond the ends of the blocks a distance that equals the sum of the thickness of the metal washer, plus the wheel width, plus the shaft collar, and an additional $\frac{1}{8}$ inch.

Shape the front and the rear walls (parts 9 and 10). The rear wall is shorter by $\frac{3}{4}$ inch and has a $2\frac{1}{4}$-inch-diameter hole through which the steering column passes. Both parts are attached with glue and 7d box nails—the front wall is butt-jointed at the end of the bed, and the rear wall has nails driven up from the bottom of the bed.

THE STEERING MECHANISM

The parts that are required for steering and their relationships are shown in Detail B. Start by cutting to length the 1-inch outside diameter aluminum tube that will be the steering column. Next, cut to length the $1\frac{1}{2} \times 3\frac{1}{2}$-inch

The steering wheel and the brake handle are wrapped with black tape. The "horn" is a cap salvaged from a one-gallon bottle. Decorative touches were added with $\frac{1}{2}$-inch-wide red tape.

pieces of stock that will be the steering column supports. It's best to cut these pieces longer than necessary, so you can trim them to exact size after checking on assembly.

Don't try to drill the 1-inch-diameter holes for the steering column at a 30 degree angle. Instead, bore the holes square through the stock and then bevel the bottom end of the parts. This will "tilt" the holes to the angle needed. First make the front support (part 11), putting it in the position shown in Detail B, and secure it with glue and by toenailing with 2d box nails. Temporarily position the steering column as a guide to help you install the rear steering-column support (part 12). This part is secured with glue and toenailed at the bottom end, and a brace (part 16) is added at the top end.

Next install the steering column. Drill a $\frac{1}{8}$-inch hole through the column about $\frac{1}{2}$ inch from one end. Pass this end through the holes in the column supports, and slip on the washer and insert the cotter pin needed at the lower end. Drill the hole for the other cotter pin on assembly after slipping on the second washer.

At a point midway between the inside surfaces of the column supports, drill a $\frac{1}{16}$-inch hole through one wall of the steering column for the sheet-metal screw that will lock the steering cable.

Use the following procedure to install the cable: Use a couple of clamps to hold the front axle block in line with the front cleat. Secure an end of the cable to the left end of the axle block as shown in Detail B-2. Using very small screweyes, secure the cable by hammering the eyes so they clinch the cable. Pass the free end of the cable through its hole in the bed, and tightly wrap it clockwise about eight turns around the steering column. Pass the free end through the second hole in the bed, and while holding the cable taut, secure it to the right end of the axle block. Now drive home the sheet-metal screw so there is an equal number of cable coils on each side of it.

The next step is to make the keepers (part 14). When they are installed, the keepers hold the cable tightly and keep it from unwinding as the steering column is turned. Detail B-3 shows how to make two keepers from one block of wood. First drill the $1\frac{1}{4}$-inch hole $\frac{1}{2}$ inch deep, and then make the 1-inch hole through the stock. Cut the piece on the centerline, and install the keepers as shown in Detail B, with the ties (part 15) which are held in place with sheet-metal screws. Before you set the keepers, place a glob of paste wax or grease on the area that bears against the cable.

Shape two pieces of $\frac{3}{4} \times$ 3-inch pieces of stock to resemble the part shown in Detail B-1. These are glued and nailed to the underside of the bed so the steering cable rides over the rounded edge. They act as guides and also serve to tighten the cable.

The hood is made from a piece of thin plastic laminate (the kind used to cover counter tops), and is secured with sheet-metal screws spaced about 2 inches apart. The laminate is easy to bend and strong enough for the job.

THE BACK ASSEMBLY

Make the two sides and the center piece (parts 19 and 20) and put them into place with glue and 6d box nails. Add the reinforcement pieces (part 21), bonding them with glue and toenailing along the top and bottom edges with 1-inch brads.

We used the kerfing method to make the back parts pliable enough to conform to the arc at the back of the bed. This is just a matter of cutting saw-blade-wide grooves across the short dimension of the pieces. Make the grooves' depth a little more than half the material's thickness and space them about $\frac{1}{2}$ inch apart. It will pay here to do the kerfing on a test piece. The closer the kerf spacing the easier it will be to make the bend. When you are satisfied with results, make the parts and put them into place with glue and 3d box nails driven between the kerfs. If you wish, you can cover the kerfs with a thin veneer that you bond with contact cement.

The top trim is made from a length of $\frac{1}{2}$-inch-diameter hose (or something similar) that you slit and then press into place. Secure the hose with 2d nails where it makes contact with the sides and the center piece.

Now make the brake handle support and the foot rests (parts 24 and 25).

These are shaped as shown in Details D and E and are attached with glue and screws in the positions shown on the main drawing. Be sure the notch in the brake handle support lines up with the slot that is through the bed.

Before going further, mount the wheels on the axles. First put on a metal washer, then the wheel, and then the wheel lock, which is a ready-made, $\frac{1}{2}$-inch-bore shaft collar.

THE BRAKE SYSTEM

Make the assembly consisting of the shoe bar and shoe shown in Detail F. A good way to make the shoes is to mark an 8-inch-diameter circle on a suitable-size piece of stock, and form the notches needed for the bar before you saw the piece to produce two shoes. Attach the bar with glue and with a single screw.

Clamp the assembly to the bed so that the shoe lines up with the wheel and the bar is centered under the $\frac{5}{16}$-inch carriage bolt hole. Drill through the hole in the bed to form the matching hole in the bar.

Next make the brake handle, shaping the top end with rasp and sandpaper to a reasonably round form. Drill the pivot hole ($\frac{5}{16}$ inch), and then mount the handle by tapping in the $\frac{1}{4}$-inch dowel pivot. The pivot should fit tightly in the holes that are in the brake handle support.

Now you can make the ties (part 30). Connect them at the handle end with a $\frac{1}{4}$-inch bolt and lock nut, and at the shoe bar end with a sheet-metal screw. We used aluminum U-channel for the ties, but you can substitute strips of $\frac{1}{4}$-inch-thick maple or birch.

The positions of the stops (part 33) and springs (part 32) are shown on the top view of the main drawing. Attach the stops with glue and a small nail or screw. Attach the springs to small screweyes that you place in the rear axle block and the shoe bar. We made the springs by cutting lengths from a screen door spring and then working with pliers to form hooks at the ends. The length of the springs should provide enough tension to keep the shoe bar snug against the stop.

The shape of the brake shoe conforms to the circumference of the wheel. The neutral-position clearance is maintained because of the springs that connect between the shoe bar and the rear axle block. Stops, which are attached to the underside of the bed, keep the springs from pulling the shoes too far forward.

The bumper was metalized with self-adhesive aluminum tape. The headlights have fronts of the same material. The letters are self-adhesive, from a stationery store. The hood louvers are strips of black tape.

THE STEERING ASSEMBLY

All the parts required for the steering assembly are shown in Detail G. Make the hub, and after drilling through it to pierce the steering column, secure it with four *panhead* sheet-metal screws set 90 degrees apart.

Shape the steering wheel and its hub, and clamp them in the correct position to a flat surface so that you can mark perpendicular diameters across both pieces. Using the marks as a guide, drill through the wheel and into the hub. Drill pilot holes first, and then enlarge them to $\frac{1}{4}$ inch. Of course, you can do the job on a drill press by holding the parts with a vise or clamp and using the blade from a square, or something similar, to align the drill with the diameter marks on the work.

Put the pieces together by adding the four $\frac{1}{4}$-inch dowel spokes and then attaching the assembly to the steering column hub with four screws. Finally, make an assembly of the plug and the horn. The plug should be sized to fit tightly in the steering column hole.

HEADLIGHTS AND BUMPER

Fashion the bumper from a piece of $1\frac{1}{2} \times 3\frac{1}{2}$-inch stock, attaching it by drilling a pilot hole and enlarging it to a depth of about $2\frac{3}{4}$ inches with a $\frac{1}{2}$-inch bit. Coat mating surfaces with glue, and then drive home the two screws. Seal the holes by gluing on two $\frac{1}{2}$-inch wood buttons.

The headlights can be cut from lumber, or you can slice them from a round or large dowel. It is not critical that the diameter be the listed size. Attach the pieces, after drilling a centered pilot hole, with glue and 5d box nails.

project 38
No-Gas Car

MATERIALS LIST

Part No.	Name	Pieces	Size	Material
1	bed	1	$\frac{3}{4} \times 16 \times 39\frac{3}{4}''$	plywood
2	rear axle block	1	$1\frac{1}{2} \times 3\frac{1}{2} \times 18''$	lumber
3	front cleat	1	$1\frac{1}{2} \times 1\frac{3}{4} \times 18''$	"
4	washer	1	$\frac{1}{4} \times 4''$ dia.	temp. harboard
5	front axle block	1	$1\frac{1}{2} \times 1\frac{1}{2} \times 18''$	lumber
6	steering post	1	$\frac{3}{4}''$ O.D. $\times 4\frac{1}{8}''$	aluminum tubing
7	washer	1	$\frac{3}{4}''$	metal
8	lock	1	$\frac{3}{4}''$ bore	shaft collar
9	front wall	1	$\frac{3}{4} \times 10 \times 10''$	plywood or lumber
10	rear wall	1	$\frac{3}{4} \times 9\frac{1}{4} \times 10''$	"
11	front steering column support	1	$1\frac{1}{2} \times 3\frac{1}{2} \times 7''$	lumber
12	rear steering column support	1	$1\frac{1}{2} \times 3\frac{1}{2} \times 9\frac{1}{2}''$	"
13	steering cable	1	$\frac{1}{8} \times 36''$	wire cable
14	keepers	2	$1\frac{1}{4} \times 3\frac{1}{2} \times 4''$	lumber
15	ties	4	$\frac{1}{4} \times 2 \times 2\frac{1}{4}''$	plywood
16	brace	1	$\frac{3}{4} \times 3\frac{1}{2} \times 5''$	lumber
17	steering column	1	$1''$ O.D. $\times 18''$	aluminum tubing
18	hood	1	$10 \times 26''$	plastic laminate

Back Assembly

Part No.	Name	Pieces	Size	Material
19	sides	2	$\frac{3}{4} \times 4 \times 6''$	lumber
20	center	1	$\frac{3}{4} \times 6 \times 6''$	"
21	glue blocks	3	$1\frac{1}{2} \times 2 \times 2''$	"
22	backs	2	$\frac{1}{4} \times 6 \times 15''$	hardboard
23	trim	1	$\frac{1}{2} \times 32''$	hose (or similar)
24	brake handle support	1	$1\frac{1}{2} \times 3\frac{1}{2} \times 7''$	lumber

Part No.	Name	Pieces	Size	Material
25	foot rest	2	$1\frac{1}{2} \times 3\frac{1}{2} \times 7\frac{1}{2}''$	lumber

Brake System

Part No.	Name	Pieces	Size	Material
26	shoe bar	2	$1 \times 1 \times 10\frac{1}{4}''$	lumber
27	shoe	2	$1\frac{1}{2} \times 3 \times 5\frac{1}{2}''$	"
28	brake handle	1	$1 \times 1 \times 11''$	"
29	brake handle pivot	1	$\frac{1}{4} \times 4''$	dowel
30	ties	2	$\frac{1}{2} \times 12\frac{1}{2}''$	aluminum channel
31	spring ties	4	$\frac{1}{4}''$	screweyes
32	springs	2	(see text)	
33	stops	2	$\frac{1}{2} \times \frac{1}{2} \times \frac{1}{2}''$	lumber
34	rear axle	1	$\frac{1}{2} \times 23''$	bar stock
35	front axle	2	$\frac{1}{2} \times 10\frac{1}{2}''$	"
36	wheels	4	$8''$ dia.	ready-made
37	wheel locks	4	$\frac{1}{2}''$ bore	shaft collars
38	headlights	2	$1\frac{3}{4}''$ dia. $\times 1''$	lumber
39	bumper	1	$1\frac{1}{2} \times 3\frac{1}{2} \times 14$	"
40	screw cover	2	$\frac{1}{2}''$	wood button

Steering Assembly

Part No.	Name	Pieces	Size	Material
41	column hub	1	$1\frac{1}{2} \times 2\frac{1}{2}''$ dia.	lumber
42	steering wheel	1	$\frac{3}{4} \times 8''$ dia.	lumber or plywood
43	steering wheel hub	1	$\frac{3}{4} \times 2\frac{1}{2}''$ dia.	lumber
44	spokes	4	$\frac{1}{4} \times 3\frac{1}{2}''$	dowel
45	plug	1	$1 \times 1\frac{1}{4}''$	"
46	cap (horn)	1	recycle a bottle cap	

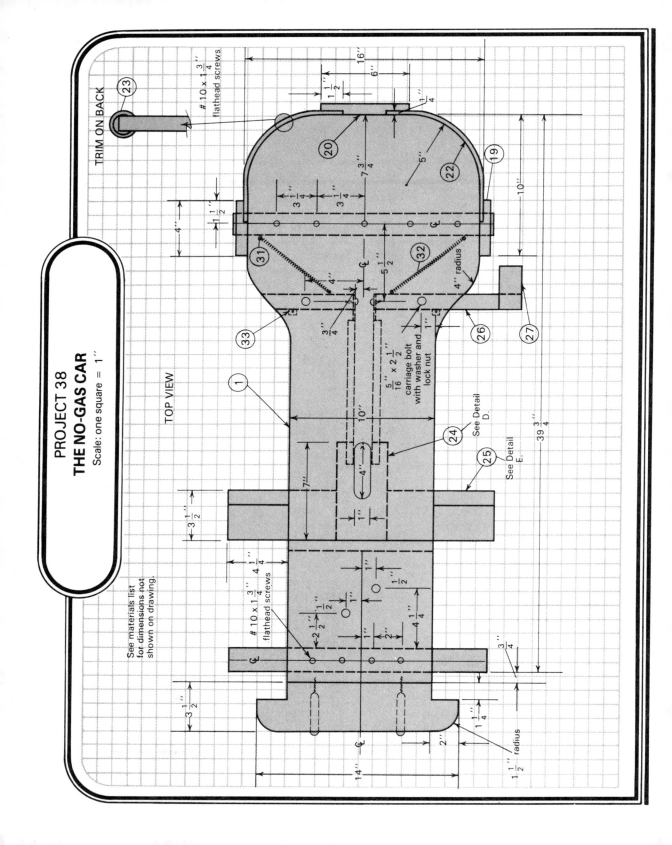

PROJECT 38
THE NO-GAS CAR
Scale: one square = 1″

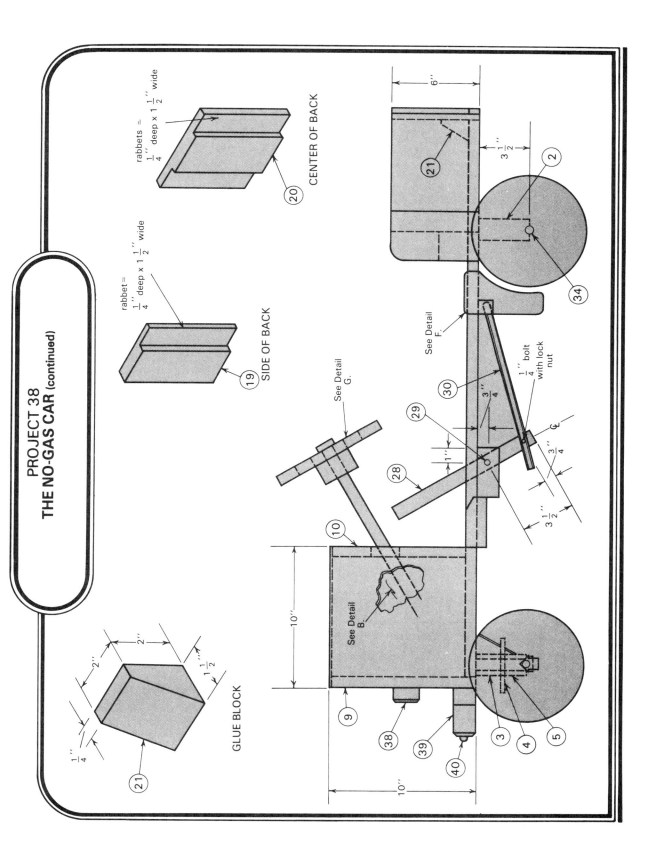

PROJECT 38
THE NO-GAS CAR (continued)

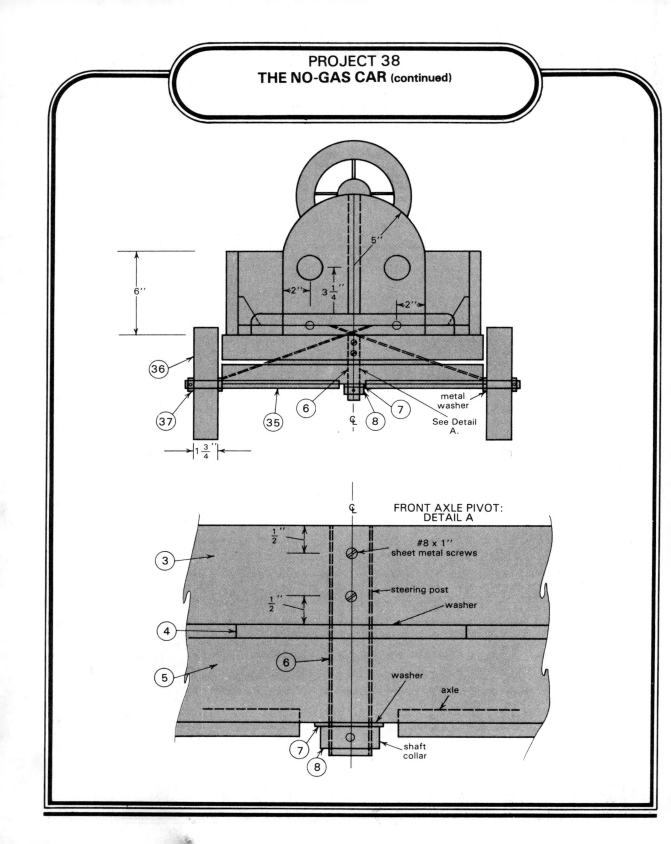

FRONT AXLE PIVOT:
DETAIL A

PROJECT 38
THE NO-GAS CAR (continued)

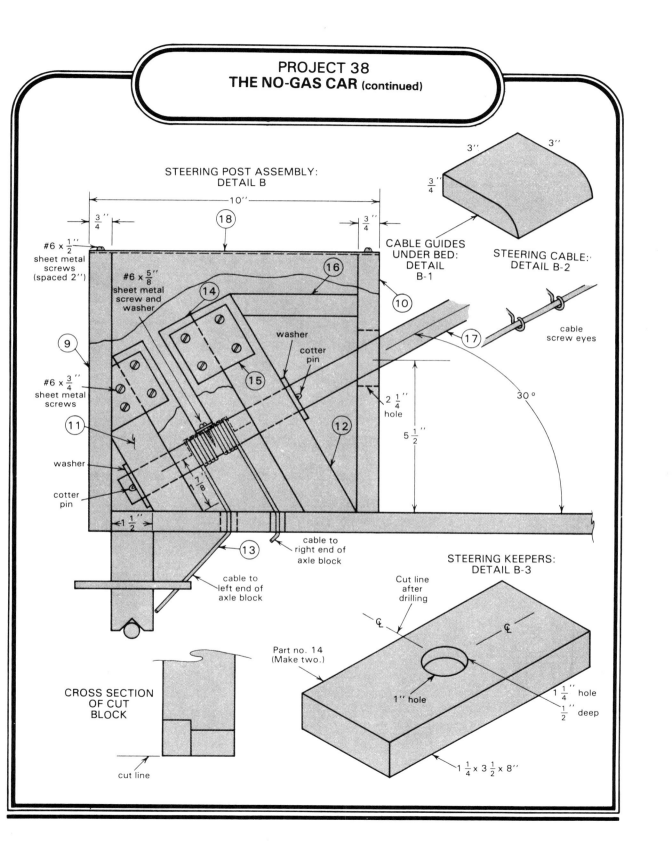

STEERING POST ASSEMBLY:
DETAIL B

10''

18

3/4''   3/4''

#6 x 1/2''
sheet metal
screws
(spaced 2'')

#6 x 5/8''
sheet metal
screw and
washer

CABLE GUIDES
UNDER BED:
DETAIL
B-1

16

14

10

STEERING CABLE:
DETAIL B-2

3''   3''

3/4''

cable
screw eyes

washer

cotter
pin

9

17

#6 x 3/4''
sheet metal
screws

15

2 1/4''
hole

5 1/2''

11

12

30°

washer

7/8''

cotter
pin

1 1/2''

13

cable to
right end of
axle block

cable to
left end of
axle block

STEERING KEEPERS:
DETAIL B-3

Cut line
after
drilling

CROSS SECTION
OF CUT
BLOCK

Part no. 14
(Make two.)

1'' hole

1 1/4'' hole
1/2'' deep

cut line

1 1/4'' x 3 1/2'' x 8''

PROJECT 38
THE NO-GAS CAR (continued)

BRAKE HANDLE SUPPORT:
DETAIL D

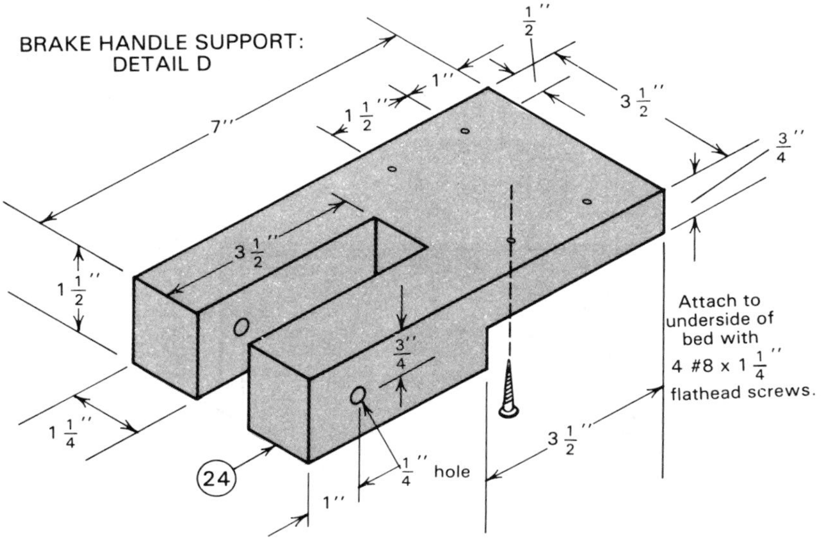

7″
1″
$\frac{1}{2}$″
$3\frac{1}{2}$″
$1\frac{1}{2}$″
$\frac{3}{4}$″
$3\frac{1}{2}$″
$1\frac{1}{2}$″
$\frac{3}{4}$″
Attach to underside of bed with 4 #8 x $1\frac{1}{4}$″ flathead screws.
$1\frac{1}{4}$″
24
$\frac{1}{4}$″ hole
1″
$3\frac{1}{2}$″

FOOTREST:
DETAIL E

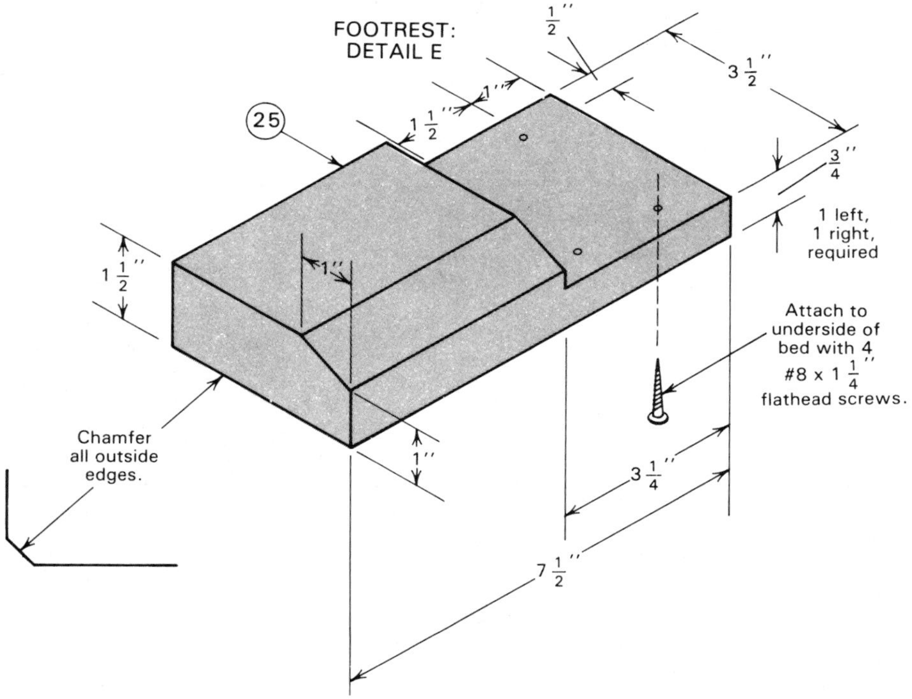

$\frac{1}{2}$″
$3\frac{1}{2}$″
1″
25
$1\frac{1}{2}$″
$\frac{3}{4}$″
1 left, 1 right, required
$1\frac{1}{2}$″
1″
Attach to underside of bed with 4 #8 x $1\frac{1}{4}$″ flathead screws.
Chamfer all outside edges.
1″
$3\frac{1}{4}$″
$7\frac{1}{2}$″

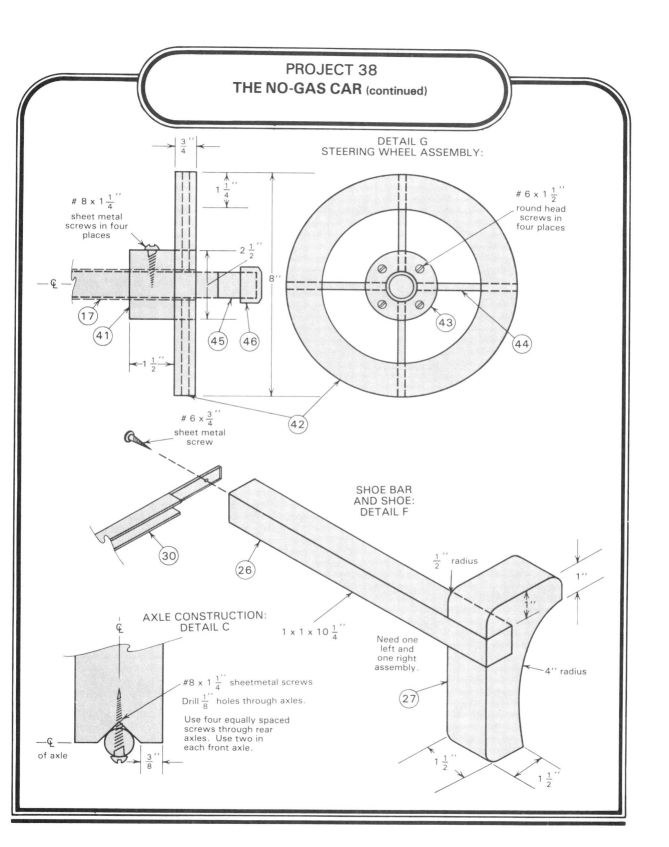

PROJECT 38
THE NO-GAS CAR (continued)

DETAIL G
STEERING WHEEL ASSEMBLY:

$\frac{3}{4}''$

$1\frac{1}{4}''$

#8 x $1\frac{1}{4}''$
sheet metal
screws in four
places

#6 x $1\frac{1}{2}''$
round head
screws in
four places

$2\frac{1}{2}''$

8''

C̶L̶

⑰

㊶

㊺ ㊻

㊸

㊹

$1\frac{1}{2}''$

#6 x $\frac{3}{4}''$
sheet metal
screw

㊷

SHOE BAR
AND SHOE:
DETAIL F

$\frac{1}{2}''$ radius

1''

1''

㉚

㉖

$1 \times 1 \times 10\frac{1}{4}''$

Need one
left and
one right
assembly.

4'' radius

AXLE CONSTRUCTION:
DETAIL C

C̶L̶

#8 x $1\frac{1}{4}''$ sheetmetal screws

Drill $\frac{1}{8}''$ holes through axles.

Use four equally spaced
screws through rear
axles. Use two in
each front axle.

㉗

C̶L̶
of axle

$\frac{3}{8}''$

$1\frac{1}{2}''$

$1\frac{1}{2}''$

Index

Auger bit, 29
Axle holes, for toys, 72–74
Backsaw, 12–13
Bar clamp, 55
Bastard cut, 45
Belt sander, 49
Bench rule, 11
Bit brace, 28
Block plane, 44–45
Box nails, 22–25
Brads, 26
Bug (car), 162–165
Bus, 168–169
Cab, 148–153
Car, No-Gas, 256–273
Carriage bolt, 60
C-clamps, 52
Circle cutters, 75–76
Clamp fixtures, 54–55
Clamps, 52–56
Claw hammer, 22
Combination square, 11
Common nails, 22–25
Common softwood, 5
Coping saw, 13, 16
Countersinking, 39
Countersink screw. *See* flathead screw
Coarse cut, 45
Crocodile pull toy, 144–147
Crossbanding, 8
Crosscutting, 12–13
Dachshund pull toy, 106–109
Dog with waggly ears pull toy,
    120–123
Dowels, cutting, 67–72
Dragon pull toy, 104
Drills
    bit brace, 28
    drill points, 28
    electric, 30–34
    hand, 27–28
Elephant with nodding head pull toy,
    124–127
Expansive bits, 30
Express wagon, 228–237
FAS (hardwood), 6
Ferris wheel, pull toy, 132–139

Files, 45–46
Finishing nails, 23, 26–27
Firsts (in hardwood), 6
Flathead screw, 35, 39–41
Fly cutters, 75–76
Folding rule, 10
Formers, 47–48
Games
    marble ride, 204–211
    marble roller coaster, 212–221
    single-post, 190–192
    spiral game, 196–199
    tick-tack-toe board and men, 184–
        189
    triple-post, 193–195
    zigzag traveler, 200–203
Glues, 56–57
Grooves, decorative, 75–78
Hacksaw, 21
Half rounds, 67–68
Hammers and nails, 22–27
Hand drills, 27–28
Hand rails, 67–68
Handscrews, 53–54
Hardwood
    definition of, 4
    grades of, 6
    thicknesses, 6–8
Hardwood plywood, 8
Hippo pull toy, 101
Hole saws, 74–75
Hopping bunny pull toy, 110–113
Jig
    center-drilling, for toy wheels, 72–74
    for cutting dowels, 68–69
    sanding, for toy wheels, 48–51
Jigsaw, 19–21
Keyhole saw, 18
Kiddie car riding toy, 238–245
Log carrier, 148–153
Lumber
    appearance of, 4
    buying, 5–8
    part size, 4
    types of, 4–5
    use of, 4
    wear and tear, 5
Lumber-core plywood, 8
Marble ride game, 204–211
Marble roller coaster game, 212–221

Measuring and marking devices
  bench rule, 11
  combination tap square, 11
  folding rule, 10
  pencil compass, 11
  tape, 10
  trammel, 12
  wing dividers, 11
Mitre box, 13–15
"Moto-Saw," 21
Moving van, 154–158
Nails
  box, 22–25
  casing, 23, 26
  common, 22–25
  finishing, 23, 26–27
  nail set, 23, 27
Novelty wheels, 81–82
Nuts, bolts, and washers, 56–60
Oval-head screw, 35, 39–41
Pad sander, 49
Patterns, copying, 61–62
Pencil compass, 11
"Piercing" cut, 13, 16
Pinwheel pull toy, 140–143
Planes, 43–44
Plug cutters, 40, 42–43
Plywood, 8
"Poles" See closet rods
Polyurethanes, 63–64
Pull toys, with action
  bunny, hopping, 110–113
  crocodile, swivelling, 144–147
  dog with waggly ears, 120–127
  drummer, rolling, 128–131
  ducks, walking, 114–119
  elephant with nodding head, 124–147
  Ferris wheel, 132–139
  pinwheel, 140–143
Pull toys, basic
  dachshund, 106–109
  dragon, 104
  puppy, 97–100
  spotty dog, 103
  whale, 102
Quarter rounds, 67–68
Rasps, 45–46
Riding toys
  kiddie car, 238–245

  rocking horse, 246–255
Ripping, 12
Rocking horse riding toy, 246–255
Rolling drum push toy, 128–131
Roundhead screw, 35, 39–41
Rounds, 67–68
Sabre saw, 18–19
"Salad bowl finish," 63
Sandpaper, 48–51
Saws
  backsaw, 13–14
  coping, 12–13
  crosscut, 12–13
  hacksaw, 21
  jigsaw, 19–21
  keyhole, 18
  rip, 12
  sabre, 18–19
Screwdrivers and screws, 35–40
Second cut, 45
Seconds (hardwood), 6
Selects (hardwood), 6
Shelving bin, 6
Single-post game, 190–192
Smooth cut, 45
Smooth plane, 43–44
Softwood, 4–6
Softwood plywood, 8
Spiral game, 196–199
Spiral ratchet screwdriver, 35–36
Sports car, 166–167
Spotty dog pull toy, 103
Spring clamps, 52–53
Structural softwood, 5
Surform tools, 47–48
"Sweep," 28
Tick-tack-toe board and men, 184–189
Tools
  clamps, 52–56
  drills, 27–35
  files, 45–46
  glues, 56–57
  hammers and nails, 22–34
  measuring and marking devices, 9–12
  nuts, bolts, and washers, 56–60
  planes, 43–44
  rasps, 45–46
  sanders, 49
  sandpaper, 48–50

saws, 12–21
screwdrivers and screws, 35–40
Toys, pull
    bunny, 110–113
    bus, 168–169
    cab and log carrier, 148–153
    cars, 162–167, 238–245, 256–273
    crocodile, swivelling, 144–147
    dogs, 97–100, 103, 106–109
    dragon, 104
    ducks, walking, 114–119
    drum, rolling, 128–131
    elephant with nodding head, 124–127
    Ferris wheel, 132–139
    hippo, 101
    pinwheel, 140–143
    rocking horse, 126–155
    sand carrier, 158–161
    trains, 170–173
    van, 154–157
    wagons, 222–237
    whale, 102
Trains, 170–183
Trammel, 12
Triple-post game, 193–195
Trucks and cars
    bug (car), 162–165
    bus, 168–169

cab and log carrier, 148–153
    moving van, 154–158
    sand carrier, 158–161
    sports car, 166–167
V-block holder, 16–17
Veneer-core plywood, 8
Vise, 16
Wagons
    express, 228–237
    toy-tote, 222–237
Walking ducks pull toy, 114–119
Whale pull toy, 102
Wheels and axles, for toys
    assembly, 86–93
    axle holes, drilling, 72–74
    axles, finishing ends of, 94–95
    dowels, cutting, 67–72
    rims, 78–80, 83–86
    wheels, making, 74–78, 80–82
Wing dividers, 11
Wood
    dimensions of, 6–7
    smoothing, shaping and finishing, 43–51
    species of, 3–5
Woodworker's vise, 55–56
Zigzag rule, 10
Zigzag traveler game, 200–203